D1458702

S

From Art Nouveau
to Deconstructivism

Klaus Richter

Prestel

Munich · London · New York

Frank Lloyd Wright, Fallingwater, Pennsylvania, 1936–37

This volume in the Prestel SightLines series is devoted to 20th-century architecture, from Art Nouveau to Deconstructivism. Reviewing its development brought home two key characteristics in particular. Firstly, architecture is not a hermetically sealed discipline, and secondly, it transcends national boundaries. Major architects of the past century built all over the world. Their nationality is irrelevant; what counts is their work.

The first section of the book, a **Glossary of Names and Concepts** lists in alphabetical order the great architects who designed the century's major buildings and helped to shape 20th-century architecture. It also gives definitions of 150 specialist terms, many of which are illustrated with drawings (p. 5).

The following section is devoted to **Styles, Tendencies, Schools and Groups**. It contains chronological descriptions, beginning in the last third of the 19th century, of twenty-three different tendencies. Many were interrelated, while others led in entirely new directions. Each entry lists the names of the key exponents and is accompanied by an illustration of a typical example (p. 24).

The **main section** of the book consists of a chronological guide, in texts, photographs and drawings, to fifty key 20th-century structures. The section is split up into the ten decades of the century, revealing which buildings were erected concurrently, and which architects were contemporaries (p. 34).

At the end of the volume, a **timeline** sets developments in architecture in the wider context of world history (p. 155).

A

Aalto, Alvar, Finnish architect (1898–1976) One of the outstanding architects of the 20th century, who designed buildings all over the world, notably the Sanatorium, Paimio, and the Opera House, Essen.

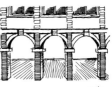

arch

abutment Top surface of a wall or support on which another structural part rests (beam, roof, etc.).

aluminum Lightweight, non-rusting metal used in modern architecture as facade cladding, roofing, light structural frameworks, and window and door frames.

architrave 1. A beam resting on columns. 2. A frame around a doorway or window.

Ando, Tadao (b. 1941) Japanese architect who continues the tradition of the Japanese house into the contemporary period. His works include the Church on the Water, Tomamu; Church of the Wind, Kobe; Church of Light, Osaka (see pp. 138–39); and the Vitra Conference Building, Weil am Rhein, Germany. Pritzker Prize, 1995.

arcade 1. Row of arches on the same plane supported on columns. 2. A top-lit roofed passage with stores along each side.

Art Deco (French: *art décoratif*, decorative art) Style fashionable in the 1920s and 1930s in industrial design, interior design and architecture. Characterized by geometrical forms and strong coloring. One of the best-known Art Deco buildings is the Chrysler Building in New York.

arch Curved structure spanning an opening in a masonry wall. Types of arch include round, pointed, ogee, etc.

architectural drawing Graphic depiction of a planned building. Such drawings were formerly done by hand, but are increasingly made with the aid of a computer.

Art Nouveau (also Jugendstil, Modern Style, Stile Liberty, Modernismo) Style prevalent in architecture and the decorative arts between 1890 and 1910 (see p. 24).

Arts and Crafts 19th-century English movement advocating the unification of the arts and handicrafts, with the aim of improving living conditions.

Asplund, Gunnar (1885–1940) Swedish architect whose use of glass, metal and other contemporary materials influenced the development of modern architecture. Outstanding works include District Court, Sölvesborg; City Library, Stockholm; and the extension to the City Hall, Göteborg.

atrium 1. Inner courtyard of a Roman house. 2. Central hall in a building several stories in height, usually with a glazed roof.

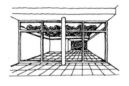

attic story (In Classical architecture) story over main entablature of a building.

auditorium A hall for the gathering of an audience, as in a school, university, etc.

axis Imaginary straight line running through the length (longitudinal axis) or breadth (transverse axis) of a building. Other axes are central axis, window axis, door axis.

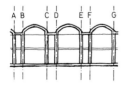

axonometric projection Three-dimensional representation showing a building from three sides. In the type illustrated (**isometric**

projection), the ground plan lies at an angle of 30° or 60° to the horizontal and is drawn to scale, while the elevations are foreshortened.

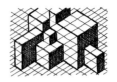

B

Bakema, Jacob Berend (1914–1981) Dutch architect and city planner who maintained a fruitful partnership with J. H. van den Broek. He described himself as a functionalist and emphasized structure in his designs. Well-known examples are the Lijnbaan Center, Rotterdam, and the large housing projects Pampusplan and Buikslotermeer, Amsterdam.

balcony A platform projecting outside the upper floor of a building and enclosed by a railing or balustrade.

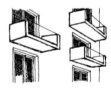

Baldessari, Luciano (1896–1982) Italian architect. One of the more unconventional representatives of Italian Rationalism.

balustrade A railing held up by small posts or columns (balusters).

Baroque Style in art and architecture prevalent from about 1600 to 1770. Characterized principally by vital, energy-charged sculptural forms and curved lines which

balustrade

were also used in ground plans. Painting and sculpture were incorporated to create a grand overall effect.

Bartning, Otto (1883–1959) German architect and theorist, designer of the twin-spire, steel-frame Melanchton-Stahlkirche (Steel Church) in Essen.

basement Bottom floor of a building, lying partly below ground level.

Bauhaus German design school, founded in Weimar in 1906. Headed from 1919 by Walter Gropius, it became the most important and influential design school of the 20th century (see p. 26).

bay Regular structural subdivision of a building, as in a church.

bay-window Projection from a building mostly filled with windows.

beam Load-bearing horizontal element of wood, steel, concrete or stone.

Behnisch, Günther (b. 1922) German architect best known for his work at the Munich Olympiapark, designed in collaboration with engineer Frei Otto. Other works include buildings in the Bonn administration district, in particular the Plenary Hall of the Bundestag, and Sankt Benno High School in Dresden.

bracket/plate Devices used to join building components.

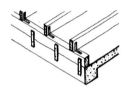

Behrens, Peter (1868–1940) German architect and designer known particularly for major industrial buildings such as the AEG Turbine Factory, Berlin.

Berg, Max (1870–1947) German architect. His most famous building was the Centennial Hall, Breslau (see pp. 44–45).

Berlage, Hendrik Petrus (1856–1934) Dutch architect whose Amsterdam Bourse became a symbol of emergent modern architecture (see pp. 36–37).

Bill, Max (1908–1999) Swiss architect and teacher. Best known for his Hochschule für Gestaltung (High School for Construction), in Ulm, Germany, where he was director from 1951 to 1956.

bitumen Semi-liquid tar product used as a sealant.

Bofill, Ricardo (b. 1939) Spanish architect known for large apartment buildings in Spain and France whose facades are decorated with classical motifs (e.g. Palacio d'Abraxas, Paris).

Böhm, Gottfried (b. 1920) German architect, son of church architect Dominikus Böhm. His reputation was established with such sculptural concrete buildings as the Pilgrimage Church, Neviges, and the City Hall, Bensberg. Pritzker Prize 1986.

Botta, Mario (b. 1943) Swiss architect. His numerous villas in Tessin are characterized by their superb integration into the environment.

Breuer, Marcel (1902–1981) Hungarian architect and Bauhaus teacher. Known for furniture designs and his collaboration on the UNESCO Building, Paris.

brick Oblong block shaped of clay and fired in a kiln to increase its resistance to weathering.

Brinkmann, Johannes Andreas (1902–1949) Dutch architect. Achieved international renown for his Van Nelle Tobacco Factory in Rotterdam (see pp. 72–73), one of the major industrial buildings of the 20th century.

Broek, Johannes Hendrik van den (1898–1978) Dutch architect. With Bakema, jointly supervised the reconstruction of downtown Rotterdam after World War II. Further works include the large Pampusplan and Buikslotermeer housing developments in Amsterdam.

Brutalism Movement initiated by Le Corbusier and characterized above all by the use of *béton brut*—raw, unfinished concrete (see p. 29). New Brutalism was a British offshoot.

building code Rules and regulations governing the design and construction of a building.

building law Legal rules concerning building, e.g. property laws, land laws, building regulations, planning regulations.

Burnham, Daniel Hudson (1846–1912) American architect, a pioneer of steel-frame high-rise construction and city planning. His best-known buildings include the Reliance Building, Chicago, and the Fuller Building, the first skyscraper in New York (see pp. 38–39). His Burnham Plan for Chicago was a farsighted and influential piece of city planning.

C

CAD (computer-aided design) The design of products or buildings with the aid of computers.

Calatrava, Santiago (b. 1951) Spanish architect best known for his spectacular bridges and train stations, such as the Satolas TGV Station, Lyon.

Candilis, Georges (b. 1913) Aberzaijan-born, French naturalized architect known for his city planning, notably at Casablanca (with Bodiansky and Woods).

cantilever A projecting beam or structure supported at only one end, which is anchored to a pier or wall.

capital The top part of a column or pilaster.

Charter of Athens Manifesto drafted in 1933 during the fourth CIAM meeting. It recommended dividing cities into separate zones devoted to the activities of living, leisure, work and transport.

Chicago School Group of architects working mostly in Chicago in the last quarter of the 19th century. Their creation of high-rise buildings featuring fire-resistant metal skeleton structures and elevators paved the way for the modern skyscraper (see p. 23).

CIAM (Congrès Internationaux d'Architecture Moderne). Association of leading architects, founded in 1928 (see p. 27) and devoted to the dissemination of the International Style.

Classicism The principles underlying the art and architecture of Greek and Roman antiquity (see **Neoclassicism**).

colonnade Row of columns capped by a continuous beam (architrave).

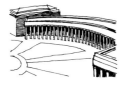

column Cylindrical upright building member, resting on a base and topped by a capital, used to support upper parts of a building.

concrete Building material comprising cement, sand, gravel and water, poured into formwork, where it sets. See also **reinforced concrete**.

conservatory A room enclosed in glass, serving to store and display plants, especially those subject to frost damage.

Constructivism Movement in art and architecture that emerged in Moscow in 1915 and subsequently influenced De Stijl and the Bauhaus. Constructivist architects demanded the abandonment of all traditions and historical principles, in favor of architecture that emphasized the utilitarian and functional aspects (see p. 26).

Coop Himmelb(l)au Group formed in 1968 by Austrian architects Wolf D. Prix (b. 1942), Helmut Swiczinsky (b. 1944), and Rainer Michael Holzer (who left the group in 1971). Their Deconstructivist designs represented an audacious alternative to conventional architecture. The best-known example is the attic conversion on Falkestrasse, Vienna (see pp. 136–37).

coping The top horizontal edge of a wall, to which a rain gutter may be attached.

corbel A small projection from a wall supporting an arch, beam, parapet, etc.

cornice A projecting horizontal molding crowing the top of a building.

Costa, Lucio (1902–1998) Brazilian architect who designed the plan for the new city of Brasilia.

courtyard An open area enclosed by walls or buildings.

curtain wall 1. Part of a straight wall between two protruding structures (buttresses, piers). 2. (In modern architecture) a thin, non-load-bearing wall of aluminum, glass, steel, etc. supported by the building's structure.

D

Deconstructivism Architectural trend heralded in 1988 by the exhibition "Deconstructivist Architecture" (MoMA, New York). It is characterized by fragmented, angled, or distorted volumes, as well as other unconventional types of structure and form (see p. 31).

Deutscher Werkbund Association of German artists, artisans, architects and manufacturers founded in 1909 (see p. 25).

Dinkeloo, John Gerard (1918–1981) American architect and co-founder of the firm Roche & Dinkeloo, whose best-known building was the Ford Foundation Headquarters in New York (1963–68).

Doesburg, Theo van (1883–1931) Dutch artist and co-founder of the De Stijl group. He taught at the Bauhaus and exerted a considerable influence on modern architecture.

dome (also cupola) A hemispherical roof built over a circular or sometimes square plan.

E

Eames, Charles (1907–1978) American designer. He is best known for his furniture, designed in collaboration with his wife, Ray, and his house at Pacific Palisades, an important example of industrialized architecture.

École des Beaux-Arts French school of architecture and art influential in the 18th and 19th centuries.

ecological architecture Method of building employing natural, sustainable materials and energy-saving technologies.

Eesteren, Cornelius van (1897–1988) Dutch architect and member of De Stijl. Collaborated in 1920–23 with van Doesburg on housing projects. President of CIAM from 1930 to 1947.

Eiermann, Egon (1904–1970) German architect. Major works include the German Embassy, Washington, D.C., the IBM Headquarters, Böblingen, and the Olivetti Building, Frankfurt.

Eisenman, Peter (b. 1932) American architect and theorist. His buildings include the Miller House, Lekeville, Conn., the Frank House, Cornwall, Conn., and the Wexner Center for the Visual Arts, Columbus, Ohio.

eclecticism Use of stylistic elements from past periods in a building design.

elevation 1. A scale drawing of the front, rear or side of a building on a plane vertical to the horizon. 2. Any external facade.

entablature In the Classical orders, the entire mass of horizontal members (architrave, frieze and cornice) supported by a column.

Expressionism Art style which flourished between 1910 and 1925 in northern European countries. Expressionist buildings are characterized by their free, sculptural and sometimes angular forms (see p. 25).

Eyck, Aldo van (b. 1918) Dutch architect working in a Structuralist style (e.g. Municipal Orphanage, Amsterdam).

F

facade Visible exterior face of a building, particularly the front.

fanlight (also lunette) A semicircular window over a door.

Fehn, Sverre (b. 1924) Norwegian architect. His works in Norway include the Glacier Museum, Fjaerland, and the Archeological Museum, Hamar. Pritzker Prize 1997.

Figini, Luigi (1903–1984) Italian architect who worked in partnership with Gino Pollini from 1929. Their residential and factory buildings for Olivetti in Ivrea are major works of Italian Rationalism.

filling/infill In timber-framed buildings, filling of gaps between the members of a frame, e.g., paneling, sticks and clay (wattle and daub), brick.

formwork A structure of wood or metal into which liquid concrete is poured and which is removed after the concrete has dried. Employed for foundations, walls, supports and ceilings, and usually made on site by carpenters.

Foster, Sir Norman (b. 1935) English architect and engineer, a leading representative of High Tech architecture. His projects include the Hong Kong and Shanghai Bank, Hong Kong, the Carré d'Art gallery, Nîmes, the Reichstag, Berlin, and the Great Court, London (see pp. 150–51).

foyer Entrance hall or lobby, especially in a theater, hotel, or apartment house.

Fuller, Richard Buckminster (1895–1983) American architect and engineer. He invented the Dymaxion House, which drew on automobile and aircraft construction techniques, and developed the geodesic dome (Expo '67, Montreal).

Functionalism Style in modern architecture based on the notion that form should be determined by function alone (see p. 24).

G

gable The triangular wall enclosed by a pitched roof.

gallery 1. Large internal passage in Elizabethan or Jacobean houses often used to display pictures and tapestries. 2. Tribune over the aisles in a church. 3. An arcaded or colonnaded passage.

garden city Concept devised in England at the turn of the 20th century by Ebenezer Howard, who advocated the creation of new, self-contained towns in the country. The first garden city was at Letchworth, Hertfordshire (see pp. 50–51).

Gaudí, Antoni (1852–1926). Catalan architect. His best-known buildings are characterized by unusual, expressive, sometimes surreal forms, and by rich decoration. One of his most famous buildings is the Church of Sagrada Familia in Barcelona, that has remained unfinished to this day.

Gehry, Frank O. (b. 1929) American architect and major representative of Deconstructivism. His spectacular Guggenheim Museum in Bilbao is one of the most famous buildings of the 20th century. Pritzker Prize 1989.

golden section Proportion consisting of a line divided in two line parts so that the ratio of the whole to the larger part is the same as the ratio of the larger part to the smaller. It has been used as an aid to determine harmonious proportions in architectural design.

Gothic Architectural style prevalent in Europe from the 12th to the 16th centuries and characterized by soaring verticality, pointed rib-vaults, pointed arches, piers formed of multiple columns and flying buttresses.

Gowan, James (b. 1923) Scots architect. He worked in partnership with James Stirling, with whom he designed the Engineering Building, University of Leicester (see pp. 112–13).

Graves, Michael (b. 1934) American architect. Major buildings include the Public Services Building, Portland, Oregon, and the Humana Tower, Louisville.

Grimshaw, Nicholas (b. 1939) British architect. He has designed a number of large metallic High Tech buildings, including the Waterloo International Railway Terminal, London; the Western Morning News Building, Plymouth; and the Eden Project, Cornwall (see pp. 152–53).

Gropius, Walter (1883–1969) German architect, theorist and teacher. Founder of the Bauhaus, Gropius was one of the leading pioneers of the International Style. Major works include the Fagus Factory, Alfeld-an-der-Leine (see pp. 52–53); the Bauhaus Building, Dessau; the Graduate Center, Harvard University; and the Pan Am Building, New York.

ground plan Horizontal section through a building, indicating position and dimensions of the rooms, etc.

Guimard, Hector (1867–1942). French Art Nouveau architect. Key works include Castel Béranger, Paris, and various Metro entrances in Paris characterized by their organic forms.

H

Hadid, Zaha (b. 1950) Iraqi-born architect. One of the major proponents of Deconstructivism (e.g. Fire Department Building, Vitra Company, Weil-am-Rhein).

half-timbering Type of construction consisting of an exposed framework of wooden beams, the spaces between which are filled with clay or brick.

Henselmann, Hermann (1905–1995) Leading architect of the German Democratic Republic, Chief Architect of East Berlin.
Hertzberger, Herman (b. 1932) Dutch architect. Major exponent of Structuralism (e.g. Centraal Beheer office building, Apeldoorn).
High Tech Style of architecture that emerged in the 1980s and emphasized the technical and structural aspects of buildings in their external appearance (see p. 31).
Hilberseimer, Ludwig (1885–1967) German architect. Teacher at the Bauhaus, and from 1938 in the U.S. He was one of the pioneers of the International Style.
Historicism (also Revivalist architecture) Architecture strongly influenced by past styles. The revival of historical styles was particularly prevalent in the second half of the 19th century.
Hoffmann, Josef (1870–1956) Austrian architect whose Palais Stoclet in Brussels marked a high point in Art Nouveau architecture.
Höger, Fritz (1877–1949) German Expressionist architect. Best known for the Chilehaus, Hamburg.
Hollein, Hans (b. 1934) Austrian architect and designer. Various retail store interiors in Vienna brought him international renown

in the mid-1960s. He also designed the Museum Abteiberg, Möchengladbach (see pp. 122–23). Pritzker Prize 1985.
Horta, Victor (1861–1947) Belgian Art Nouveau architect. Major works include Hôtel Tassel and Maison du Peuple in Brussels.

I

industrial architecture Architecture of manufacturing plants. An important, separate form of modern architecture in the 20th century.
industrialized building Construction method using prefabricated elements that are assembled on site.
International Style Name coined in 1932 for a style of architecture in America and Europe characterized by cubic building volumes, flat roofs, horizontal window bands and parapets, white stucco facades, and lack of ornamentation (see p. 27).
isometric projection Method of perspective drawing showing a building. Slightly distorted, but more realistic than an axonometric projection.
Isozaki, Arata (b. 1931) Leading Japanese architect. Buildings include MoMA, Los Angeles, and the Team Disney Headquarters, Buena Vista, Fla.

J

Jacobsen, Arne (1902–1971) Danish architect influenced by the International style. Also known for his refined furniture designs.
Jahn, Helmut (b. 1940) German-born American architect. Known

13

for his large hotel and office buildings (e.g. Messeturm, Frankfurt, and Sony Center, Berlin).

Johnson, Philip (b. 1906) American architect. Student of Gropius and Marcel Breuer at Harvard. Initially an exponent of the International Style, he later veered into Postmodernism (e.g. AT&T Building, New York; see pp. 132–33) and Deconstructivism. Pritzker Prize 1979.

joist Any of the parallel beams that hold up the planks of a floor, the laths of a ceiling, or the covering of a roof.

K

Kahn, Albert (1869–1942) German-born American architect known for his industrial buildings.

Kahn, Louis I. (1901–1974) American architect. The National Assembly of Bangladesh in Dacca (see pp. 116–17) is one of the highlights of a prolific career.

keystone The topmost stone, set last, in a masonry arch or vault.

Kikutake, Kiyonori (b. 1928) Japanese architect and member of the Metabolist group (see p. 106).

Klerk, Michel de (1884–1923) Dutch architect known for his housing developments and residential architecture. His most interesting project is Het Scheep, Amsterdam (see pp. 56–57).

Koolhaas, Rem (b. 1944) Dutch architect, advocate of Deconstructivism. Works include the Netherlands Dance Theater, The Hague, the Contemporary Art Museum, Rotterdam, and the Grand palais and master plan for Euralille, France.

Kurokawa, Kisho (b. 1934) Japanese Metabolist architect. Works include the Sony Tower, Tokyo; the Japanese-German Center, Berlin; and the International Airport, Kuala Lumpur, Malaysia.

L

lantern A small round superstructure over an opening in a ceiling or vault.

Le Corbusier (Charles-Édouard Jeanneret-Gris, 1887–1965). Swiss architect active in France. One of the most influential architects and theorists of the 20th century. Works include the Villa Savoye, Poissy; the Unité d'Habitation, Marseille (see pp. 88–89); and the Pilgrimage Church, Ronchamp.

Libeskind, Daniel (b. 1946) American architect of Polish origin. Created a masterpiece of Deconstructivist architecture with his Jewish Museum, Berlin (see pp. 146–47).

lintel A beam over an opening in a wall or over two or more pillars or posts.

Lissitzky, El (1890–1941) Russian architect and graphic designer.

lintel

Leading figure in Constructivism. Famous for his Lenin Tribune (1920), a steel framework rising diagonally into the air.

Loos, Adolf (1870–1933) Austrian architect. He advocated architecture stripped of all ornament (*Ornament und Verbrechen* [Ornament and Crime], 1908). His work was Neoclassical in spirit.

lunette 1. Part of a wall under a semicircular vault. 2. Fanlight. 3. A fortification with two faces forming a projecting angle.

Lutyens, Sir Edwin (1869–1944) English architect known for his beautiful country estates in the Arts and Crafts style.

M

Mackintosh, Charles Rennie (1868–1928) Scottish architect and designer. His buildings exerted a profound influence on the Arts and Crafts movement and Art Nouveau.

Maki, Fumihiko (b. 1928) Japanese architect. One of the founding members of Metabolism in Japan. Pritzker Prize 1993.

marble A hard, metamorphic limestone, white or variously colored, streaked or mottled due to the admixture of minerals.

masonry Stonework.

May, Ernst (1886–1970) German architect planner. Director of Town Planning and Building in Frankfurt-am-Main, 1925-30, where he designed the Römerstadt Housing Development.

megastructure Large, enclosed complex of buildings, often housing various functions.

Meier, Richard (b. 1934) American architect. His pristine white residences and museum buildings have made him one of the best-known contemporary architects (see pp. 124–25). Pritzker Prize 1984.

Melnikov, Konstantin (1890–1974) Russian architect. Best known for his workers' club-houses in Moscow, especially the Rusakov Club (see pp. 62–63).

Mendelsohn, Erich (1887–1953) German architect. His early work was Expressionist (Einstein Tower, Potsdam), but his later designs were influenced by the International Style.

Metabolism (Greek: change, transformation) Japanese movement founded in 1960 by a group of architects and city planners. Their aim was to ease urban congestion and expand cities by adopting innovative types of structure (see p. 30).

Meyer, Adolf (1881–1929) German architect. Close collaborator of Gropius from 1911–25, and teacher at the Bauhaus from 1919–25.

Mies van der Rohe, Ludwig (1886–1969) German architect, emigrated to the U.S. in 1938. He was one of the most influential exponents of the International Style. Major buildings include the Barcelona Pavilion, the Seagram Building, New York, and the Neue Nationalgalerie, Berlin.

Modernism Radical movement in 20th-century architecture aimed at breaking with past architectural styles, emphasizing the importance of producing rational solutions to contemporary needs using modern materials. The International Style was its most important manifestation.

modular architecture Type of construction employing prefabricated elements based on standard units of measurement (modules), to lower costs and increase efficiency of the building process.

Modulor System of proportions invented by Le Corbusier in 1951. Based on the golden section, and a human height of 1.83 meters (6 feet).

Moneo, Rafael (b. 1937) Spanish architect. He has designed various buildings in Spain, as well as the Museum of Art and Architecture, Stockholm. Pritzker Prize 1996.

Moore, Charles (b. 1925) American architect. A leading Postmodernist, he has created a diverse body of work, including St. Joseph's Fountain on Piazza d'Italia, New Orleans.

mortar Mixture of cement or lime with sand and water, used to fill joints in masonry or stone walls.

museum architecture An independent building genre since the founding of the British Museum in London (1753). In the 20th century, museum buildings were among the largest architectural projects in Europe.

Muthesius, Hermann (1861–1927) German architect. A co-founder of the Deutscher Werkbund, he was an advocate of mass-production and industrialization. He collaborated on the planning of the first German garden city, Hellerau, near Dresden.

N

National Socialist architecture Architectural trend linked with the Nazis' political demand for a "new German architecture," based on Historicism and characterized by propagandistic aims.

Neoclassicism Major architectural style that emerged in European and American art in the 18th century, based on a return to the Classicism of antiquity. There was a resurgence of Neoclassicism in the 20th century through the International Style and Postmodernism (see p. 24).

Nervi, Pier Luigi (1891–1979) Italian architect and engineer. He is best known for his reinforced concrete structures covering unusually large spans. The soaring, weightless effect of his designs is exemplified by the Palazzetto dello Sport, Rome (see pp. 98–99).

Neutra, Richard (1892–1970) Austrian architect. He emigrated to the U.S. in 1923. Known for spacious private residences in the International Style.

New York Five A group of architects—Peter Eisenman, Michael Graves, Charles Gwathmey, John Heyduk and Richard Meier—who came together following an exhibition of their work in New York in 1969. They were known as the "Whites" because of their predilection for white buildings in the International Style.

Niemeyer, Oscar (b. 1907) Brazilian architect. He was appointed Chief Architect to the new city of Brasilia, where he designed the Cathedral, the Palaces of the Three Powers and the Government Buildings. Pritzker Prize 1988.

Nouvel, Jean (b. 1945) French architect. His works include the Institut du Monde Arabe and the Fondation Cartier, Paris; the Galeries Lafayette, Berlin; and the Cultural and Convention Center and Art Museum, Lucerne.

O

Olbrich, Joseph Maria (1867–1908) German architect and a prominent figure in the Vienna Sezession. His major work is the complex of buildings at the Mathildenhöhe artists' colony, Darmstadt.

Otto, Frei (b. 1925) German architect and engineer. A pioneer in the field of suspended roof construction, renowned for the tent roof at the Olympiapark in Munich (see pp. 114–15).

Oud, Jacobus Johannes Pieter (1890–1963) Dutch architect. Founding member of De Stijl, best known for significant residential buildings and public housing schemes, including a row of houses for the Weissenhofsiedlung exhibition in Stuttgart.

P

parapet A low wall or railing, as along a balcony.

parquetry Inlaid woodwork in geometric forms used especially in flooring. Laid over planking or poured concrete.

pavilion Free-standing, light, usually single-story building in a park or pedestrian zone.

Pei, Ieoh Ming (b. 1917) American architect of Chinese origin. The Pei Office is one of the largest architectural firms in the U.S.

Buildings include the Hancock Tower, Boston; Bank of China, Hong Kong; and the Pyramid at the Louvre, Paris (see pp. 134–35). Pritzker Prize 1983.

Pelli, Cesar (b. 1926) American architect of Argentine origin. Well-known works include the World Financial Center, New York, and the Petronas Towers, Kuala Lumpur.

penthouse floor Top floor of a building, sometimes set back from the main facade, occupied by a penthouse.

Perrault, Dominique (b. 1953) French architect. Achieved international recognition for his Bibliothèque Nationale, Paris.

Perret, Auguste (1874–1954) French architect, a pioneer of reinforced concrete (skeleton frames). His buildings in this material include the Church of Notre-Dame, Le Raincy (1922–24)

perron Platform reached by symmetrical flights of steps.

Piano, Renzo (b. 1937) Italian architect. His buildings include the Centre Georges Pompidou, Paris (with Rogers), the Menil Collection Building, Houston, and Kansai Airport (see pp. 140–41). Pritzker Prize 1998.

pier A stout pillar or column, or a vertical member in a metal or concrete building frame.

pilaster A half, or slightly raised, column or pillar on a wall surface.

pillar An upright support, usually of square or rectangular section, that carries the upper part of a building.

Poelzig, Hans (1869–1936) German architect. Best known for his IG Farben Building, Frankfurt-am-Main.

Ponti, Gió (1891–1979) Italian architect and designer. His major work is the Pirelli Building, Milan.

portico A large porch set before the facade of a building, usually consisting of a pediment supported by columns.

Postmodernism Term used since the late 1970s to describe new tendencies in architecture that rejected the strict functionalism of the International Style in favor of eclecticism and pluralism (see p. 30).

posttensioning Technique used to make reinforced concrete, in which the steel is run through ducts created in the concrete. When the concrete has hardened, the steel is anchored and stretching force is applied. The process increases the tensile strength of the concrete. See **pretensioning**.

prefabrication Production of buildings in standardized sections to be assembled on site. Used primarily for large buildings consisting of many, repetitive elements, such as walls, ceilings, facade sections, balconies, bathrooms, etc.

pretensioning Technique used to make reinforced concrete. Lengths of steel are stretched and anchored before the concrete has been poured. Once it has set, the anchors are released and the steel compresses the concrete. Prestressed concrete achieves strength without the aid of heavy steel reinforcements, permitting lighter, shallower and more elegant structures.

Pritzker Architecture Prize The "Nobel Prize for Architecture," donated by Jay A. and Cindy Pritzker and endowed with $100,000, awarded annually since 1979 in recognition of an individual architect's achievement by the Hyatt Foundation.

proportion The comparative size relation between separate parts of a building, and between these and the whole.

R

Rationalism A form of architecture based on the rejection of ornamental, Historicist styles in favor of supposedly logical principles (see p. 28).

raw concrete Rough, unfinished concrete, as it comes from the formwork, used as a design element. Its surface can be worked, e.g. by washing out the fine components (washed concrete) or by means of stonemason's tools.

reinforced concrete Concrete in which iron or steel rods or mesh are encased to increase its tensile strength.

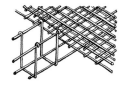

rendering Drawing in which elevations of buildings, views of streets, squares or interiors are depicted in context.

Ridolfi, Mario (1904–1984) Italian architect. He was essentially a Rationalist, although his INA Casa in Rome was more eclectic in style.

Riemerschmid, Richard (1868–1957) German architect and interior designer. Collaborated with Tessenow and Muthesius on the first German garden city, Hellerau, near Dresden.

Rietveld, Gerrit Thomas (1888–1964) Dutch architect and designer. His Schröder House,

Utrecht, was a superb translation of the ideas of the De Stijl movement into architectural form.

Roche, Eamonn Kevin (b. 1922) American architect of Irish origin. Projects done in collaboration with his partner, John Dinkeloo, include the Ford Foundation, New York. Pritzker Prize 1982.

Rogers, Richard (b. 1933) English architect, a leading exponent of High Tech architecture. His buildings include the Centre Georges Pompidou, Paris (with Piano), the Lloyd's Building, London (see pp. 128–29), and the European Court of Human Rights, Strasbourg.

Romanesque Architectural style prevalent in Western Europe between 900 and 1150. It is characterized by massive walls and piers, semicircular arches, barrel vaults and simple geometrical plans.

Rossi, Aldo (b. 1931) Italian architect and theorist. His Modena Cemetery buildings are outstanding examples of Rationalist architecture. Also known for his School in Broni (see pp. 126–27). Pritzker Prize 1990.

Rudnev, Lev Vladimirovich (1885–1956) Russian architect whose Lomonosov University in Moscow (see pp. 86–87) set new standards for Soviet architecture and urban planning.

S

Saarinen, Eero (1910–1961) Finnish-born American architect. His early work was in the International Style (General Motors Center, Warren), but later work is characterized by sweeping, expressive forms (TWA Terminal,

Kennedy International Airport, New York).

Safdie, Moshe (b. 1938) Israeili-Canadian architect. His best-known project is the Habitat modulor housing development in Montreal for Expo '67.

scale Size of a drawing or model in relation to the actual size of thing represented. The most common scales in architecture are 1:1, 1:5, 1:10, 1:20, 1:50, 1:100, 1:200, 1:500, and 1:1000.

Scarpa, Carlo (1906–1987) Italian architect and designer. His most notable works include the Brion Cemetery, San Vito d'Altivole near Treviso, and the Banca Popolare, Verona.

Scharoun, Hans (1893–1972) German architect. Early in his career he became known for housing developments. He adopted an expressive, organic style, exemplified by his famous Philharmonie, Berlin (see pp. 100–1)

Schütte-Lihotzky, Margarete (1897–2000) Austrian architect. She developed the Frankfurt Kitchen, which became the model for contemporary built-in kitchens.

Sezession (known as Jugendstil in Austria) Term adopted by groups of artists in Germany and Austria during the 1890s to mark their secession from the traditional academies.

Shreve, Richmond Harold (1877–1946) American architect. Designer of the Empire State Building, New York.

Siza Vieira, Álvaro (b. 1933) Portuguese architect. He has designed a variety of buildings and housing projects. Portuguese pavilion for Expo '98 in Lisbon. Pritzker Prize 1992.

Skidmore, Owings & Merrill American architectural firm best

known for its commercial sky-scrapers, such as Lever House, New York, and the John Hancock Center and Sears Tower, both in Chicago.

skyscraper Tall, multi-story building. The first examples were built in American in the 1880s. Made possible by the invention of the elevator and the skeleton structure of steel or reinforced concrete. Initially served as office buildings; residential high-rise buildings did not emerge until the early 1930s.

Smithson, Alison (1928–1933) and Peter (b. 1923) British husband-and-wife team. Their most successful project is the Economist Building, London (see pp. 104–5).

socle Base-course of a wall.

span The distance from one support to the next, as between bridge piers.

street furniture Objects erected in the street for public use, such as streetlamps, benches and post-boxes.

Speer, Albert (1905–1981) German architect and Hitler's chief architect. His planned redesign of Berlin, with broad axes and bombastic buildings, was prevented by World War II.

Stam, Mart (1899–1986) Dutch architect and designer. Collaborated with Poelzig, Taut, and May, as well as Brinkmann and van der Vlugt (Van Nelle Tobacco Factory, Rotterdam).

Stirling, James (1926–1992) Scots architect. He is best known for the Staatsgalerie, Stuttgart. Pritzker Prize 1981.

string A narrow horizontal strip of masonry projecting slightly from a wall.

structural engineering The calculation of the stability of a structure by determining the forces at

string

work within it and the required strength of its parts. Structural engineers work closely with architects.

Structuralism The employment of a system of order (grid) for all architectural disciplines, from town planning to individual houses (see p. 29).

Sullivan, Louis Henry (1856–1924) American architect of Irish, Swiss and German origin. In his best-known buildings, such as the Wainright Building, St. Louis, and the Guaranty Building, Buffalo, the skeleton frame is exposed on the outside.

T

Tange, Kenzo (b. 1913) Japanese architect and planner. His buildings have a sculptural quality (e.g., Yamanashi Press and Broadcasting Center, Kofu, and New City Hall, Tokyo). Pritzker Prize 1987.

Tatlin, Vladimir (1885–1953) Russian architect, painter and sculptor. Known for his Monument to the Third International.

Taut, Max (1884–1967) German architect. Designed two houses for the Weissenhofsiedlung, Stuttgart, and one of the first high-rise apartment houses in Berlin.

Terragni, Giuseppe (1904–1941) Italian architect. A pioneer of modern architecture in Italy and a leading Rationalist. His most famous project is the Casa del Fascio in Como (see pp. 76–77).

Tessenow, Heinrich (1876–1950) German architect and reformer in the field of housing. He planned the first German garden city, Hellerau, near Dresden.

totalitarian architecture The officially prescribed architecture in totalitarian countries between 1930 and 1945. During this period modern architecture was suppressed and replaced by a style approved by the regimes.

truss Supporting framework for various types of roof. Usually made of wooden beams, but when longer distances are to be spanned, steel or reinforced concrete are used.

U

Ungers, Oswald Mathias (b. 1926) German architect. His exhibition and museum buildings have made him one of the leading contemporary architects in Germany.

Utzon, Jørn (b. 1918) Danish architect. The Sydney Opera House is his most famous work (see pp. 108–9).

V

Vago, Pierre (b. 1910) French architect and long-time editor of the periodical *L'Architecture d'aujourd'hui.*

vault An arched roof or ceiling made of stone, brick or concrete. Types of vault include barrel, groined, sexpartite, and star.

Velde, Henry van de (1863–1957) Belgian architect and designer, a leading figure in Art Nouveau.

vault

at various sites in the Midwest and California sites, Fallingwater in Pennsylvania (see pp. 80–81), and the Guggenheim Museum, New York.

Y

Yamasaki, Minoru (b. 1912) Japanese architect and designer known above all for the World Trade Center, New York.

Z

Zumthor, Peter (b. 1943) Swiss architect, supervisor of historical monuments and university professor. The Thermal Baths in Vals, Canton of Graubünden, and the Kunsthaus, Bregenz, are his best-known projects.

Venturi, Robert (b. 1925), American architect and theorist, one of the founders of Postmodernism. One of his earliest buildings was the Vanna Venturi House, Philadelphia (see pp. 110–11). Pritzker Prize 1991.

Vesnin, Alexander (1883–1959) Russian architect. With his brothers Leonid (1880–1933) and Viktor (1882–1950), he ran a successful practice during the Constructivist period, concentrating particularly on workers' clubs and theater buildings.

virtual architecture The use of data processing in designing and constructing buildings. Also, the three-dimensional projection of a design in space (see p. 32).

Vlugt, Leendert Cornelius van der (1848–1936) Dutch architect who worked on the Van Nelle Factory, Rotterdam.

W

Wagner, Otto (1841–1918) Influential Austrian architect. His early buildings were in a Historicist vein (Majolikahaus, Vienna), but he later adopted a less ornate style, exemplified by his Post Office Savings Bank, Vienna (see pp. 48–49).

Wright, Frank Lloyd (1867–1959) American architect. One of the most influential architects of the 20th century. His most famous projects include the Prairie Houses

1870 Chicago School

A group of architects active in Chicago who played a key role in the development of the skyscraper. Before the Great Fire of 1871, wood was the predominant building material in Chicago. Following the fire, there was a need to rebuild rapidly in fireproof materials and architects began experimenting with metal frameworks or skeleton structures. This construction technique also provided a significant gain in rentable area over masonry at a time when there was growing pressure on land values in the city. This revolutionary building method, along with the invention of the elevator, permitted office and commercial buildings to rise to unprecedented heights. At first, architectural design lagged behind technological advances. Building facades continued to be richly ornamented in a way that concealed rather than reflected the modern load-bearing frame within. Then, in 1887, the

Holabird & Roche, Tacoma Building, Chicago, 1887

thirteen-story Tacoma Building went up in Chicago. It was the first skeleton structure whose functional elements were visible from the outside: vertical piers, horizontal spandrels marking the floor beams, and large-area windows in between.

Architects of the period:
Daniel Hudson Burnham, Holabird & Roche, William Le Baron Jenney, John Wellborn Root, Louis Henry Sullivan

1890 Art Nouveau, Jugendstil

Variously known as Art Nouveau, Stile Liberty or Stile Floreale (in Italy), Modernismo or Estilo Modernista (in Spain) and Jugendstil (in Germany). The German term

Antoni Gaudí, Casa Milá, Barcelona, 1906–10

derived from the magazine *Jugend*, which was designed in and reported on the new style. Its origins went back to the Arts and Crafts movement in England, which was directed against the prevailing imitation of historical styles. The Art Nouveau style was characterized by ornamentation derived from natural forms in nature, such as tendrils, waves or flames, although abstract shapes like circles, curves, ellipses and

23

spirals were also employed. This architectural idiom would later spawn great innovations despite the fact that it remained a transitional phenomenon of the decades between 1890 and 1910.

Architects of the period:
Antoni Gaudí, Hector Guimard, Josef Hoffmann, Victor Horta, Charles Rennie Mackintosh

1900 Functionalism

This term was derived from a phrase used by the American architect Louis H. Sullivan in an 1896 essay: "Form Follows Function." This renowned, often-quoted dictum became the credo of a number of modern architects, encapsulating the theory that architectural form should be determined by function alone. It represented a rejection of historicism, as well as the ornamentation of such styles as Art Nouveau. The Bauhaus would later raise Functionalism to the first principle of architecture. In the period of reconstruction following World War I, German architects made it the basis of a straightforward, unornamented, highly cost-

Walter Gropius, Fagus Factory, Alfeld-an-der-Leine, 1911–13

effective architectural style, especially in the field of housing. Functionalism has also been equated with such unfortunate developments as the proliferation of boring box-like structures seen in postwar social housing developments on both sides of the Atlantic.

Architects of the period:
Peter Behrens, Walter Gropius, Adolf Loos, Ludwig Mies van der Rohe, Louis Henry Sullivan

1900 Neoclassicism

An architectural style based on ancient Greek and Roman examples. It originally flourished in the second half of the 18th century, but it underwent a revival in the 20th century. It can be seen in certain buildings in the Scandinavian countries, in Germany and Italy during the nationalist and Fascist

Gunnar Asplund, District Court, Sölvesborg, 1917–21

period, and Stalinist architecture in the Soviet Union. More recently, Neoclassical elements played a key role in Postmodernism. The continuing fascination for Neoclassicism among architects testifies to the perennial appeal of the simplicity, rigor, order and rationality of Greek and Roman architecture.

Architects of the period:
Gunnar Asplund, Peter Behrens,
Edwin Lutyens, Heinrich
Tessenow

1907 Deutscher Werkbund

An association of German architects, designers, artisans, artists
and manufacturers who, under the
motto "honesty to materials," set
out to improve the design of
domestic appliances and furnishings. Exhibitions, publications and
lectures were used to disseminate
the association's aims, which had
much in common with those of
the 19th-century English Arts and
Crafts movement. Following the
German example, an Austrian
Werkbund was founded in 1912,
and a Swiss Werkbund in 1913.
The original association was dis-
banded by the Nazis in 1933. It
was re-established in 1946, but
failed to exert the same kind of
influence.

1910 Expressionism

(From the French *expression*)
Expressionist architecture flourished mostly in northern Europe
and is characterized by free,
abstract, monumental, sculptural
forms. Favored materials were
concrete and rough masonry.
An example of the early phase
is Erich Mendelsohn's Einstein
Tower in Potsdam, while a good
example of the second phase is
Le Corbusier's Chapel of Notre
Dame- du-Haut at Ronchamp.
Having no common agenda
and forming no cohesive group,
Expressionist architects remained
comparatively isolated and

Le Corbusier, Chapel of Notre-Dame-
du-Haut, Ronchamp, 1950–54

specimens of their work were few
and far between.

Architects of the period:
Fritz Höger, Michel de Klerk, Erich
Mendelsohn, Hans Poelzig

1912 Amsterdam School

A small group of Dutch architects
who worked in an imaginative and
expressive style of brick architecture (Johann Melchior von der
Mey, Pieter Lodewijk Kramer,
Michel de Klerk, et al.). Their
buildings have strongly sculptural
forms. The facades were richly
decorated with reliefs, ornaments,
friezes, and terracotta figures inset
in the masonry walls.

1917 De Stijl

This group was founded in
Holland by painters, architects
and designers who dubbed the
style they championed "Neo-
Plasticism." In architecture, this
involved designing buildings from
the inside out, taking account of
the purpose of each individual
room. This principle was first suc-
cessfully put into practice in the
Schröder House in Utrecht,
designed by Gerrit Rietveld.

25

Gerrit T. Rietveld, Schröder House,
Utrecht, 1924

Architects of the period;
Theo van Doesburg, Cornelius van
Eesteren, Jacobus J. Pieter Oud,
Gerrit Rietveld

1918 Constructivism

The Constructivist movement
emerged shortly after World War I
in Moscow and advocated the
complete rejection of all traditions
in favor of a "New Reality." Architecture was to be reduced to
absolutely necessary, functional
elements and would, like the other
arts, be subjected to the dictates of
technology. The movement's
adherents believed that a building
should consist solely of the parts
required to ensure its structural
integrity. It should be engineered
rather than designed on the basis
of aesthetic principles, which were
rejected as mere formalism. The
influence of Constructivism on
European architecture was limited
to the De Stijl group in Holland
and the Bauhaus in Germany. It is
possible to see a second phase of
Constructivism emerging in about
1950, when new construction
materials and developments in
structural engineering made new
forms possible. Constructivist

echoes can also be detected in
some High Tech and Deconstructivist buildings.

Vladimir Tatlin, Monument to the
Third International, 1919/20

Architects of the period:
El Lissitzky, Vladimir Tatlin,
Alexander, Leonid and
Viktor Vesnin

1919 Bauhaus

Established in Weimar, Germany,
the Bauhaus was a school of
design where architects, painters,
sculptors and artisans were
brought together to produce what
its founder, the architect Walter
Gropius, called "the new construction of the future." It aimed to uni-
fy art and technology. "It is not our
aim to propagate any style, system,
dogma, formula or fashion," said
Gropius, "but solely and exclusive-
ly to exert a vitalizing influence on
planning." In 1925, Gropius also

designed the new building when the school moved to Dessau. Its white, cubic volumes and rigorous layout reflected the Bauhaus ideals and made the building renowned worldwide as a shining example of modern architecture. It set the first standards for the emergent International Style. The Bauhaus became the most famous design school of the 20th century. It had many distinguished teachers and a number of great architects were trained there. It was closed down by the Nazis in 1933.

Walter Gropius, Bauhaus, Dessau, 1925/26

Architects of the period:
Marcel Breuer, Walter Gropius, Ludwig Hilbersheimer, Adolf Meyer

1922 International Style

The name of this style was given currency by the exhibition "The International Style" in New York in 1932 and the book *The International Style, Architecture since 1922*, by Henry-Russell Hitchcock and Philip Johnson, published at the same time. The style's principal traits were simple, cubic volumes; flat roofs; unornamented white facades; horizontal emphasis provided by window bands; detailed

design of entrances, forecourts and bays; and a sensitivity to site. Despite strong international similarities, the style was interpreted in many different ways, yet the

Ludwig Mies van der Rohe, Weissenhofsiedlung, House 3/4, Stuttgart, 1927

simple, clear, functional appearance of the new buildings in this style formed a worldwide standard. The ideas and theories of the International Style were kept alive for almost thirty years by the CIAM, the most important association of architects of the period.

Architects of the period:
Walter Gropius, Le Corbusier, Ludwig Mies van der Rohe

1928 CIAM

The CIAM (Congrès Internationaux d'Architecture Moderne) was an association of leading modern architects founded in 1928, after the Werkbund Exhibition in Stuttgart, by Le Corbusier in Switzerland. The aim was to gain

Le Corbusier, Villa Savoye,
Poissy near Paris, 1929–31

support for innovative solutions in architecture and city planning, and, more specifically, to disseminate the theories of the International Style. Ten CIAM congresses were held in various countries at irregular intervals between 1928 and 1956. Each meeting emphasized a certain theme, such as modern technology, building norms, efficiency, and urban planning. The fourth centered on "the functional city" and led to the publication of the Charter of Athens in 1933.

Architects of the period:
Le Corbusier, Pierre Jeanneret, Ernst May, Mart Stam

1930 Totalitarian Architecture

Between the two world wars, dictatorial governments came to power in several European nations. In Germany, Spain, Italy and the Soviet Union, modern architecture was largely suppressed. Totalitarian regimes demanded a different type of architecture, favoring monumental public buildings, shrines for the celebration of political power, and, in the field of housing, styles based on national traditions.

1931 Rationalism

This movement centered on the group known as MIAR, or Movimento Italiano per l'Architettura Razionale, an offshoot of Gruppo 7, which had been founded in 1926. MIAR followed a strict agenda: economic construction techniques, the use of prefabricated building elements, and mass production, from furniture to finished houses. Its members were convinced that designing and building on the basis of modern industrial methods would lead to an improvement in people's lives. Rationalism in a more general sense implies an adherence to the laws of logic and a search for elementary, fundamental forms. It was a recurring theme in the diverse architectural currents that ran through 20th-century architecture.

Giuseppe Terragni, Casa del Fascio, Como, 1932–36

Architects of the period:
Luciano Baldessari, Luigi Figini, Mario Ridolfi, Giuseppe Terragni

1933 Charter of Athens

At the fourth CIAM congress in 1933, on the theme of "The Functional City," Le Corbusier and the other members proposed that large cities should be divided into separate zones (for living, recreation, work and transportation). In the course of the congress, thirty-three large cities were analysed and their requirements and conditions were investigated.

1950 Brutalism

This style originated with Le Corbusier's use of *béton brut* (raw concrete), but was eventually also applied to buildings not made of concrete. Brutalist architecture displays honesty to materials and the exposure of structure and services. In the interiors, too, each structural element, including plumbing and heating pipes, was left exposed. This uncompromising display of materials was intended to show how, and of what, the building was made. Brutalism was a worldwide architectural trend in the 1950s, and it continues to influence architects to this day.

Architects of the period:
Le Corbusier, Louis I. Kahn, Peter and Alison Smithson, Kenzo Tange

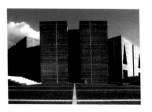

Louis I. Kahn, National Assembly, Dacca, 1968–72

1957 Interbau

The Interbau (International Building Exhibition), held in 1957 in Berlin, was the largest West German reconstruction project of the

Paul Baumgarten, Hansa Quarter, Berlin, 1956/57

postwar period. In the city's destroyed Hansa Quarter, international architects from thirteen nations erected apartment buildings in contemporary styles that set the standards for subsequent public housing in Germany—a veritable open-air design school for the country's young architects.

Architects of the period:
Luciano Baldessari, Paul Baumgarten, Van den Broek and Bakema, Pierre Vago

1960 Structuralism

In architecture, Structuralism connotes the application of a basic order to every sphere of construction, from the family house through large buildings to the planning of entire cities. The most obvious manifestation of this approach is the grid, a network of perpendicular lines over which a design is made. The structural framework of this design grid establishes an underlying order

Herman Hertzberger, Centraal Beheer Office Building, Apeldoorn, 1968–72

within which buildings, city squares, and streets are laid out. In Structuralist buildings, once the basic layout has been established, the user is then often left to develop the interior according to their own needs. Structuralism is one of the most important currents in modern architecture and urban planning. The term was first used by the architectural critic Arnulf Lüchinger to describe a contemporary Dutch style employed by Aldo van Eyck and others.

Architects of the period:
Georges Candilis, Herman Hertzberger, Moshe Safdie, Aldo van Eyck

1960 Metabolists

(From the Greek for change or transformation.) A group of Japanese architects and city planners who sought new solutions to the congestion of Japanese cities and the problems of a rapidly changing society. Their ideas included the construction of groups of towers, or even entire floating cities, and the alleviation of traffic problems by connecting new and old neighborhoods with a system of elevated streets. They considered architecture not as solid and immutable but as transformable and replace-

able. Flexibility in the use of buildings was a central element in their work. Some went as far as to propose that separate elements or even entire structures would be replaced after serving their purpose for a certain period. Although this vision was utopian, it did give rise to a number of practical and useful ideas.

Kiyonori Kikutake, Ocean Civilisation, 1959

Architects of the period:
Arata Isozaki, Kiyonori Kikutake, Kisho Kurokawa, Fumihiko Maki

1965 Postmodernism

The term Postmodernism was first used by Charles Jencks in "The Rise of a Post-Modern Architecture" (*Architectural Association Quarterly*, October–December, 1975), but the earliest signs of the trend actually appeared as early as the 1960s. A precise description of the style is impossible, because it covers a plethora of architectural forms, sometimes even within the same building. What one can say is that it marked a rebirth of eclecticism and pluralism in mod-

Charles Moore, Piazza d'Italia,
New Orleans, 1976–79

structures, composed of multiple layers and superimpositions, and their exposed frameworks reveal the articulation of stories and walls. Everything that is usually hidden inside a building is clearly displayed on the exterior. This is a style in architecture that is largely devoid of historical references.

Architects of the period:
Günter Behnisch, Frei Otto, Norman Foster, Renzo Piano, Richard Rogers, Nicholas Grimshaw

ern architecture and represented a rejection of the prevailing Modernism and Functionalism of the day, and in particular the idea that form should above all be determined by function and purpose. Postmodernists rearranged stylistic elements from the past into a new, imaginative and occasionally ironic visual idiom.

Architects of the period:
Michael Graves, Charles Moore, James Stirling, Robert Venturi

1970 High Tech

High Tech is a style based on the expression, and accentuation even, of the industrial materials, technologies and services that make up a building. Its roots can be traced back to the work of such figures as Buckminster Fuller, Frei Otto and Pierre Chareau. Technical elements such as plumbing, wiring, elevators, metal joints, nuts, bolts and rivets are left visible rather than being concealed, as in traditional architecture. High Tech buildings are open, transparent

Norman Foster, Hongkong and Shanghai Bank, 1979–86

1980 Deconstructivism

This neologism can perhaps best be defined as disintegration, destruction, and even chaos. When the concept was introduced in a New York exhibition in 1988, audiences were astonished and perplexed. These buildings expressed a totally knew visual language, aimed at the destabilization of existing architectural styles. The architects working in this idiom often play with the building components to the point of over-stepping the bounds of structural integrity, for instance by extending building volumes diagonally far beyond their center of gravity, creating an effect of instability and precariousness. Familiar architectural configurations appear unhinged, broken up for no apparent reason. Bernard Tschumi, speaking at the first International Symposium on Deconstruction in London in 1988, explained that this was not a style but part of an investigation of the dissolving borderlines of architecture. Peter Eisenman even views the approach as a way of shocking people out of the complacency of their mundane lives.

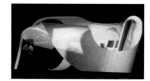

Ben van Berkel/Caroline Bos, Model of Dutch pavilion for the Milan Triennial, 1996

CAD (computer-aided design) program. Drawings are no longer made with pencil and paper on a drawing board but at the computer. Three-dimensional drawings, or perspectives, are also produced in this way. These can even be "entered," that is, one can virtually walk through the rooms on the screen. This animated representation of space is an enormous advantage when it comes to presenting an architectural project. Computer experts are currently working on the projection of three-dimensional designs into actual, full-size spaces. Soon we may be able to enter a non-existent building and experience it virtually.

Zaha Hadid, Fire Station for the Vitra Company, Weil-am-Rhein, 1989–92

Architects of the period:
Coop Himmelb(l)au, Frank O. Gehry, Zaha Hadid, Daniel Libeskind

1990 Virtual Architecture

This term was originally used to describe the planning and execution of traditional architectural tasks with the aid of computers. Nowadays, architects commonly create their drawings using a

2000 Conversions

The last years of the millennium were marked by a number of distinguished architectural projects based on conversions of, or additions to, old buildings. They ranged from opera houses (Glyndebourne, Michael Hopkins), banks (ING Bank, Budapest, Erick van Egeraat) and sports stadia (Media Centre, Lord's cricket ground, Future Systems), to parliament buildings (the Reichstag, Berlin, Foster and Partners) and art

Herzog & de Meuron, Tate Modern, 1998–2000, view from north-east with footbridge

galleries (Tate Modern, Herzog & de Meuron), What these schemes had in common was the way they reconciled a respect for the existing architecture with a bold use of space and new technology. Going beyond the sometimes facile and superficial gestures of Postmodernism, these projects heralded a new, deeper, more sensitive response to the past, without compromising the quest for innovation that is the essence of great architecture.

ESTABLISHED PAST,
SHADES OF THE FUTURE

In an age of revolutionary change that affected all areas of life, architecture experienced a precipitous development. The new building materials of iron, steel, glass and, above all, concrete opened up unprecedented possibilities for design and construction. The prevailing **Historical Revival** styles increasingly came under fire, and a search for new approaches began both in Europe and the United States. ▪ The American architects of the **Chicago School** developed what was probably the most revolutionary type of construction ever, the metal framework or skeleton, together with fire-resistant sheathing materials. The invention of the elevator played a key role in this development, for it spurred the construction of the first high-rise buildings, which would soon change the face of cities all over the world. ▪ In Europe, **Art Nouveau** emerged as an innovative architectural style. But although it engendered a number of major buildings, it remained a transitional phase that lasted only a few years. ▪ When American architect Louis H. Sullivan declared that the function of a building came first and its form would automatically follow, it marked the birth of **Functionalism** in architecture. Supplanting Historicism and Art Nouveau, this approach proved so momentous that its effects are still visible today. ▪ Yet the revival of classical styles, **Neoclassicism**, also played a role in the development of early 20th-century architecture. Models from Greco-Roman antiquity shaped the facades of public buildings and conferred prestige on the residences of prosperous private citizens. ▪ The **Deutscher Werkbund** (German Craft Association) was founded. This was an association of architects, artisans, artists and manufacturers who set out to modernize the design of objects and appliances for everyday use. ▪ The century began with the best intentions and ambitious ideas, and the results were already extremely promising.

STOCK EXCHANGE, AMSTERDAM

Architect: Hendrik Petrus Berlage

This great public building was a milestone in the history of Dutch architecture. It broke with the prevailing Historical Revival styles of the 19th century with an innovativeness that made it a model of advanced building. ■ Stylistic borrowings from the past were no longer needed. Berlage set out to reduce architecture to what was absolutely necessary and utilitarian, and to leave the construction materials visible. Those used in his Stock Exchange were primarily red brick in the walls and vaulting, iron for the trusses, hewn stone for piers and corbels, and glass in the skylights. Yet while the detailing of the elements may have been determined by technical necessity, their execution reflects outstanding craftsmanship. ■ This architecture of sweeping outlines and expansive planes would come to exert a profound influence on architecture in Europe.

The design is based on a unified grid system, applied both to floor plans and elevations. Yet although this order is clearly visible, it does not appear schematic, because subsequent construction in the area to the rear has resulted in a variety of adjoining spaces. ■ The entrance, next to the striking corner tower, leads into the great hall of the Commodities Exchange (left). Beyond this, a central passageway leads to the two smaller halls of the Grain and Stock Exchanges. Grouped around these three halls are offices, common rooms, a canteen and a post office. The spacious, open character of the interior contrasts with the solidity of the exterior with its sparing apertures. ■ The Stock Exchange is now used for exhibitions, conventions and events.

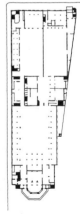

Ground floor plan

FULLER BUILDING, NEW YORK

Architect: Daniel Hudson Burnham

This building is perhaps the most famous early 20th-century American skyscraper. When it was inaugurated in 1903, it was the tallest building in the world, with 21 stories rising to a height of 87 m.
■ The developments which made possible the construction of the Fuller (or "Flatiron") Building took place some years previously: the development of fire-resistant steel frame construction for piers, walls and ceilings, and the invention of the safe passenger elevator.
■ The steel frame, or skeleton, permitted many components to be prefabricated. The skeleton was thus delivered to the site in sections, where it was then assembled, and the areas between the load-bearing elements were filled with masonry or other prefabricated, lightweight construction elements. Thanks to this method, building time was shortened and weight was saved, lowering construction costs. ■ The elevator made it possible to build higher than ever before. Access to the floors was no longer provided by staircases, which now served only as emergency access or escape routes. ■ In terms of planning, construction and utilization, the Fuller Building paved the way for future skyscrapers. Provision was made for retail stores on the ground floor, with offices, practices and apartments on the upper floors, and utilities and service areas on the top floor. The building's core contained elevators, safety stairwells, plumbing and electricity shafts, access corridors, restrooms and storage spaces. All of the rooms lay on the outside, benefiting from natural light and ventilation. Only later would separate ventilation and air-conditioning equipment become an integral part of skyscraper architecture. ■ These principles, hallmarks of the Chicago School, have remained the basis for skyscraper design to this day.

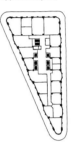

Upper floor plan

The facade of the Fuller Building is of natural stone masonry, reflecting the fashion of the day, and contrasts sharply with the innovative, modern design and construction of the interior (later skyscrapers no longer had "applied" facades of this type). ■ The building stands on a triangular lot in Manhattan that ends in an acute angle. Due to its striking shape, New Yorkers dubbed it "The Flatiron Building." The year 2001 marked the centenary of this landmark, which is still beautifully preserved. ■ The idea of raising the tallest building in the world has continued to intrigue both architects and contractors. In 1903, the title was held by the Fuller Building at 87 meters, but in 1931 it passed to the Empire State Building, also in New York, at 338 meters, a record broken in 1974 by the Sears Tower in Chicago, at 447 meters. The distinction will shortly belong to Shanghai's World Financial Center, which will be 460 meters high.

PALAIS STOCLET, BRUSSELS

Architect: Josef Hoffmann

This large and luxurious residence on the outskirts of Brussels anticipated the design of later buildings by the De Stijl group and the Bauhaus. It exemplifies the transformation that took place in architecture at the turn of the century. The rigorous design of the exterior reflects the attention that was lavished on every detail. ▪ The overall composition of the building consists of interlocking cubic volumes of various sizes, topped with an almost exotically ornamental tower. ▪ The facade is clad with white marble slabs framed by bronze elements. The windows are set at regular intervals flush with the facade, and on the top story they project above the cornice line. ▪ The architect's visual imagination is reflected in personal touches that owe nothing to past styles.

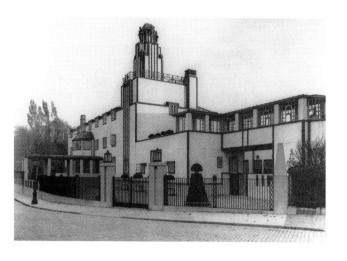

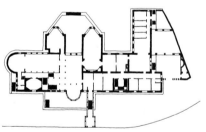

Ground floor plan

Hoffmann's masterpiece embodies an idea that has long intrigued artists and architects, that of the *Gesamtkunstwerk*, the total, inter-disciplinary work of art. The grandiose forms of the exterior, with its exquisite materials, are echoed inside, especially in the dining room, which contains mosaic murals by Gustav Klimt (left) featuring plants and figures, the culmination of the artist's "golden style."

The decor and furnishings of the rooms were based on Hoffmann's drawings and executed by the Wiener Werkstätte (Vienna Work-shops).

The Palais Stoclet is rightly regarded as one of the major buildings of the 20th century.

CASA MILÁ, BARCELONA

Architect: Antoni Gaudí

The design of this unusual apartment house is based on a combination of forms derived from nature and geometry. Together with the Church of the Sagrada Familia, the Casa Milá is Gaudí's most significant building, for it represents the apotheosis of his architectural and aesthetic ideas. ▪ The ground plan gives an impression of organic growth, as does the facade of rough-hewn stone with its rows of wavelike balconies. Every feature obeys a sculptural unity, resulting in a radical visual idiom which resists historical classification because it had neither predecessors nor successors. ▪ The ironwork railings are especially striking, dangling like proliferating vegetation over the balconies. The richness of ideas, formal variety, and craftsmanship evident in this structure remain unique. ▪ The superstructures on the roof—chimneys and ventilation ducts—have been transformed into monumental, three-dimensional forms reminiscent of a sculpture garden. Clad with fragments of tiles or shaped of fired clay, they would exert a considerable influence on 20th-century sculpture (below).

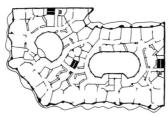

Upper floor plan

The Casa Milá lies on a street corner in the Ensanche residential area of Barcelona. The lot is rectangular, measuring 35 by 56 m. Although the building's corner is actually cut off on a straight diagonal, the semicircular balconies at the corners of the facade create the impression that it is rounded.

The apartments have no load-bearing walls, only pillars, which permit considerable flexibility of interior use. All of the corners in the rooms are rounded. Access to the apartments is provided by two main stairwells in the two interior courtyards. There are also two additional interior stairwells providing quicker access to some apartments.

The ground plan was devised with the aim of providing pleasant, comfortable living conditions. The strongly modeled exterior reminiscent of a weathered rock formation has prompted locals to nickname the building "La Pedrera" (the quarry).

CENTENNIAL HALL, BRESLAU (WROCLAW)

Architect: Max Berg

New building materials and engineering methods applied to large-scale construction projects provided great impetus to the development of modern architecture. Reinforced concrete, initially employed only in industrial buildings, was gradually used for more traditional architectural tasks. ■ The erection of the *Jahrhunderthalle*, or Centennial Hall, provided evidence of the great distances that could be spanned using concrete reinforced with an iron armature. The great circular space, uninterrupted by supports, offered a whole range of potential uses. The dome covered an area three times the size of the stone dome of St. Peter's in Rome, yet at only half its weight. ■ Being completely unclad, the structure reflected a further innovation—the use of raw, exposed cast concrete as it emerged from the timber shuttering. Le Corbusier would later make this feature a key stylistic element in his buildings and raw concrete has since become ubiquitous in modern architecture. ■ The Breslau Centennial Hall, with its self-supporting, arcuated dome, became a model for future auditoriums and exhibition halls.

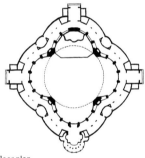

Ground floor plan

The dome measures 65 m in diameter. Unsupported by internal piers, its 32 ribs converge in a radial sweep from the lower to the upper dome ring. The ribs are intersected by bands of clearstory lights, which allow uniform daylight to penetrate. The stepped arrangement of these bands gives the exterior its striking appearance.

The dome rests on four great arches around the circumference. Between them are entrances to the four apses adjoining the central space which, depending on the use made of the hall, can be separated from it by means of curtains.

THE MODERN AGE BEGINS

The new currents in modern art, such as Expressionism, Cubism, abstraction, Futurism, Constructivism, De Stijl, Neue Sachlichkeit and the Bauhaus, all of which emerged in the first two decades of the century, had a considerable, if belated, influence on architecture. ▪ The stage for modernity was first set in Europe. **Expressionism** led to striking, freestyle, sculptural buildings in Germany and Holland, constructed in the preferred local material, brick. These were prime examples of how strong the link between fine art and architecture could be. ▪ The influence of the group of Dutch artists known as **De Stijl** led to a new approach to building in which interest focused on the requirements of separate rooms, which in turn determined the overall configuration of the final structure. ▪ **Constructivism**, developed in Russia by a group of avant-garde artists, soon spread to western Europe. At its most extreme, this style demanded that buildings should consist solely of elements absolutely necessary to their function. ▪ All of these progressive ideas converged in the program of the Bauhaus, founded in 1919. The **Bauhaus** became the most important school of art and architecture of the century. It marked the beginning of a new kind of architecture which rejected the borrowing of styles or features from the past and concentrated on new, unprecedented forms. ▪ The teachers at the school, an international group of artists and architects famous in their own right, had such a great influence on architecture, design and art that the name Bauhaus became synonymous with an entire epoch.

1904–06, **Post Office Savings Bank,**
1910–12 **Vienna**
Architect:
Otto Wagner
Pages 48–49

1910–13 **Letchworth Garden City,**
Hertfordshire
Town Planner:
Sir Ebenezer Howard
Architect:
Raymond Unwin
Pages 50–51

1911–13 **Fagus Factory,**
Alfeld-an-der-Leine
Architect:
Walter Gropius
Pages 52–53

1917–21 **District Courthouse,**
Sölvesborg
Architect:
Gunnar Asplund
Pages 54–55

1917–21 **Het Scheep Apartment Block,**
Amsterdam
Architect:
Michel de Klerk
Pages 56–57

Architect: Otto Wagner

By the time Wagner started work on the Post Office Savings Bank, he was an experienced architect. Having previously worked in the Art Nouveau and Neoclassical styles, he now decided to jettison the past entirely. Instead of continuing to apply a decorative facade to a structure, Wagner conceived the Post Office Savings Bank in terms of simple, aesthetically clear forms. It is one of the seminal works of modern architecture. ■ Its exterior is strikingly lucid, even plain, yet on second glance we see that the white marble plaques on the facade are punctuated by rows of aluminum bolts set at regular intervals, creating a finely articulated, regular pattern which breaks up the monotony of the large, flat surfaces. ■ The interior reveals the same honest approach to materials and their effects. The columns penetrate the vaulted glass roof and the unusual floor of the main hall, made of glass bricks, provides illumination for the floor below. ■ Such features reflect the architect's conviction that modern forms should be suited to the new materials used and conform to the new demands of the modern age.

Ground floor plan

The building's detailing is sparing, unobtrusive and sympathetic to the materials employed. It provides accents without impairing the overall architectural effect. The warm air exhausts, for example, have a sculptural quality and the glass floor blocks are surrounded by fine inlay work. For structural reasons, the cross section of the vertical supports decreases from top to bottom, and the pattern created by the iron framework supporting the frosted glass ceiling is echoed on the floor.

Both inside and out, the Post Office Savings Bank remains as compelling a piece of architectural design as the day it was built.

Letchworth Garden City, Hertfordshire

Town Planner: Sir Ebenezer Howard
Architect: Raymond Unwin

The social reformer Ebenezer Howard was the founder of the garden city movement and Letchworth was his first experiment to test the theories that he had outlined in *Tomorrow: A Peaceful Path to Social Reform* (1898; reissued in 1902 as *Garden Cities of Tomorrow*). The garden city was an attempt to circumvent the problems (traffic congestion, pollution, the inaccessibility of institutions and amenities, etc.) inherent in large agglomerations, with their ever-expanding suburbs. Howard advocated a new pattern of urban development based on decentralized organization and aimed at reducing the widening gap between countryside and city. Each city would be a self-contained entity, with a population of 32,000, surrounded by an agricultural belt. The land would belong to a corporation or municipality, and profits would go to the improvement of the community through lower taxes or new services. Both Letchworth and Howard's second scheme, Welwyn Garden City (from 1919), served as prototypes for the new towns built by the British government after World War II and his ideas had a far-reaching impact on town planning.

Letchworth illustrates Howard's preoccupation with separating the commercial center and the residential and industrial areas. In keeping with his choice of name for this new urban concept, the city abounds in gardens and greenery. Unlike other visionary planners and architects, such as Sant'Elia and Le Corbusier, Howard was not tied to a particular aesthetic or physical image: his main concern was to "see that our citizens are decently housed." A recognizable "garden city style" did emerge, however, influenced by the Arts and Crafts movement, which drew on vernacular and medieval themes.

FAGUS FACTORY,
ALFELD-AN-DER-LEINE

Architect: Walter Gropius

The Fagus Factory, which manufactured shoemaker's lasts, was designed at a time when Gropius was sharing an office in Berlin with his partner Adolf Meyer. He was not approached by the contractor until the plans for the building, drawn up by an experienced industrial architect, had already been submitted to the building authorities for approval. Gropius left the plan untouched, concentrating on improvements to the exterior. ■ Both the layout of the buildings and their dimensions were determined by the production process. The glass-fronted block illustrated below was an integral part of the overall plant. Strikingly functional in appearance and displaying an uncompromising use of brick, glass and steel, the Fagus Factory was a pioneering work of the International style and exerted a strong influence on other architects.

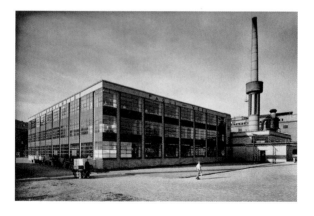

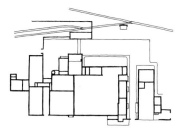

Plant layout

The Fagus Factory was the first building to demonstrate the degree of transparency that could be achieved in reinforced concrete construction. Gropius recessed the load-bearing members behind the transparent facade, and extended the glazing around the corners to produce a building volume of unprecedented lightness. The base, cornice, piers and vestibule block were executed in ocher-yellow brick, set off by dark gray window frames of fine-section steel and horizontal bands of sheet metal on the floors. The overall impression is one of extraordinary simplicity, the design deriving its beauty from perfect proportions and the balance between open and closed planes.

DISTRICT COURTHOUSE, SÖLVESBORG

Architect: Gunnar Asplund

The buildings of the Swedish architect Gunnar Asplund exemplify the advances made in modern Scandinavian architecture. Although his District Courthouse has certain Neoclassical echoes, its overall design is clear, refined, and largely devoid of historical details. Hints of Asplund's later Modernist designs can already be detected. ▪ The ground plan, however, is essentially classical and features an interesting combination of two volumes, with the cylindrical space of the courtroom being inserted into the overall rectangular volume of the building (below). The front stairway, vestibule, hall and courtroom lie along, or are accessible from, the central axis of the building. This is a hallmark of Asplund's designs, being found, for instance, in his Stockholm Public Library (1920–28) as well.

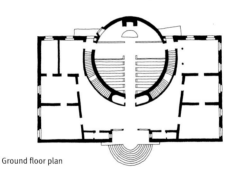

Ground floor plan

The building is given a strong unity by the repetition of circles and semicircles, from the front stairway and main entrance to the interior stairwells around the courtroom, the judge's bench and seat niche, and the courtroom windows. Many of the built-in wooden furnishings, such as the balustrade in front of the bench, the bench itself and the floor clock, have rounded or spherical elements. The severity of the design is softened by the ocher-yellow stucco facade, the white vestibule walls, and the subdued gray and yellow tones of the interior.

HET SCHEEP APARTMENT BLOCK, AMSTERDAM

Architect: Michel de Klerk

De Klerk was a member of the Amsterdam School of Dutch architects who were particularly active from 1912 to 1922. Het Scheep was one of a number of outstanding public housing projects they designed. ■ Here de Klerk was able to give free rein to his imagination and love of playful detail. His compositional skill can be seen in the design of the common area, front courtyard and interior court. The proportions of the building's volumes and surfaces were daring for their time. ■ It is perhaps unfortunate that this architecture of brick walls, tiled roofs, and broad, white-framed windows remained a Dutch idiom and found few emulators on the international stage. The scheme's key features are the sculptural articulation of the facades, the striking roofline punctuated by chimneys, and the distinctive tower. The powerful, sculptural forms and the stalagmitic tower give the building a markedly Expressionist feel.

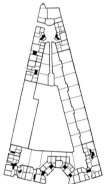

Upper floor plan

Thanks to its trapezoidal shape reminiscent of a ship's hull, the building's tenants affectionately dubbed it "Het Scheep" (the ship). ◼ Imaginative, finely crafted details abound, and the brickwork has a masterful precision and elegance. Thanks to painstaking construction and maintenance, the building is still in a perfect state of preservation despite its age.

EUROPE IN A DIALOGUE
WITH THE WORLD

The Dutch artistic movement known as De Stijl, founded in 1917, had a powerful impact on architecture in Europe between the wars. Its members advocated a paring down of art to the most basic elements: straight lines, right angles, pure planes and primary colors. ■ In the 1920s, architects abandoned the historical styles and traditions, the monolithic facades and hermetic interiors of the 19th century. Encouraged by improvements in hygiene, they began to open buildings up to air and sunlight, allowing interior and exterior space to interpenetrate. The environment, whether natural or manmade, was now taken into account in the design process. ■ A new direction in architecture, the **International Style**, emerged in Europe. Its cubic volumes, flat roofs and white facades with horizontal bands of windows would soon appear in the United States as well. ■ At the international gatherings of the **CIAM** (Congrès International d'Architecture Moderne), architects met to exchange experiences and discuss new ideas and theories. ■ **Garden cities** and **housing developments** set standards for low-income housing and soon led to the emergence of a new architectural discipline, **urban planning**. ■ The Italian group MIAR (Movimento Italiano per l'Architettura Razionale) promoted a new form of **Rationalism** in which economic construction methods and prefabrication were key elements. ■ Russian architects built in the **Constructivist** style, restricting their designs to the essential functional elements. And at the end of the decade, one of the century's greatest architects, Ludwig Mies van der Rohe, designed one of the period's most famous buildings: the German Pavilion at the 1929 Barcelona World's Fair. Thanks to the virtuoso design and the quality of the materials, this small structure would become an icon of modern architecture, admired throughout the world.

1924	**Schröder House,** **Utrecht** Architect: Gerrit Thomas Rietveld Pages 60–61	

1927–28	**Rusakov Workers' Club,** **Moscow** Architect: Konstantin Melnikov Pages 62–63	

1927–29	**Lovell Health House,** **Los Angeles** Architect: Richard Neutra Pages 64–65	

1927	**Weissenhofsiedlung,** **Stuttgart** Architects: Mies van der Rohe, Hans Scharoun, et al. Pages 66–67	

1929	**German Pavilion,** **Barcelona World's Fair** Architect: Ludwig Mies van der Rohe Pages 68–69	

SCHRÖDER HOUSE, UTRECHT

Architect: Gerrit Thomas Rietveld

With this small family house abutting a conventional row of suburban houses, Rietveld and his collaborator, the interior designer Truus Schröder, created what looked like the experimental prototype for a new form of dwelling—which it actually was. No attempt was made to adapt the structure to the adjoining houses. It remained a solitary gem, a paradigm of modern design. ▪ Rietveld was a member of De Stijl, and this house is a convincing implementation of that group's Neo-Plasticism. The basic shape of the house, a cube, was opened up and segmented by means of highly unconventional, elementary forms—planar walls, balcony slabs and railings, flat roof projections, and corner windows—and then recomposed into an aesthetically pleasing equilibrium. ▪ The three sides, painted black, white, gray and the primary colors red, yellow and blue, recall paintings by Mondrian.

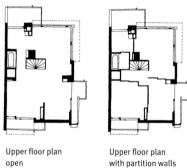

Upper floor plan
open

Upper floor plan
with partition walls

Rietveld's innovations extended to the interior as well. Flexible screens meant the entire, open upper floor could be divided into separate rooms if desired (above). Color was was also an important design element in the decor.

The interpenetration between interior and exterior space, created by walls that extend uninterrupted from the balconies into the rooms, is an aspect that would later reappear in the houses designed by Bauhaus architects.

61

Architect: Konstantin Melnikov

In the wake of World War I, the need for radical social change became increasingly apparent to Russian artists and architects, who embarked on unprecedented experimentation in the visual arts and architecture. As a result, Constructivism was born. In the realm of architecture, the term meant reducing a building to the essential functional and structural elements. ▪ The Rusakov Workers' Club, one of the few Constructivist projects actually built, perfectly fulfilled this criterion. The club was intended to serve as a public center for cultural education, and the architect underscored the importance of this purpose with an audacious design. ▪ From the central stage and auditorium, three cantilevered concrete volumes project dramatically into space. These create an impression of contained power, in keeping with the architect's description of the structure as a "tensed muscle."

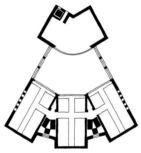

The three sections of the building can be used either separately or together to form an auditorium that seats 1,200. The walls of the interior spaces define the external shape of the structure, whose severity is mitigated to some extent by the variety of the materials—concrete, glass and brick. This reflects the Constructivist idea that a building should ultimately consist only of the structurally necessary materials and elements, without any superfluous decorative addition.

This type of architecture remained current in Russia for only a few years. It was soon supplanted by an officially prescribed Neoclassicism.

LOVELL HEALTH HOUSE, LOS ANGELES

Architect: Richard Neutra

When Richard Neutra left Austria in 1923 to work in the United States, he brought the European International Style to the New World. ■ His American career began with this house in Beverly Hills, which became the seed of Modernism and its innovative design and construction principles in America. ■ The house stands on a concrete foundation floor, and its upper stories have a light steel framework. The use of a standardized grid system gives the facades a lucid order. Every trait of the International Style is in evidence here: the simple, cubic building volume, the flat roof, the plain white facade, the horizontal emphasis of window and balustrade bands, and the integration of the architecture into its surroundings. ■ This style of architecture proved to be truly international, and is today found in hundreds of examples worldwide.

Plan of middle floor

Access to the house is by way of the top floor. All of the rooms have expansive glazed areas, which bring the outdoors right into the house. This interpenetration of internal and external space, and the interlocking levels of the living areas, resulting in open rooms of different heights, are important features of this building, which remains an exemplary piece of architectural design to this day.

WEISSENHOFSIEDLUNG, STUTTGART

Architects: Mies van der Rohe, Behrens, Gropius, Le Corbusier, Oud, Poelzig, Scharoun, Bruno and Max Taut, et al.

The Weissenhofsiedlung (literally, the "white house estate") by the Deutscher Werkbund was intended as an exhibition of workers' housing. It set the stage for modern public housing and urban planning, and contributed to the founding of the CIAM, an association of architects who met regularly to discuss current issues in modern architecture and ultimately developed the International Style. ■ The twenty-one terraced and detached houses and apartment buildings were designed by an international group of sixteen well-known architects in conjunction with Mies van der Rohe, who was responsible for overall planning. ■ The scheme broke new ground by offering adaptable, rationalized living spaces and exploiting innovative construction methods. It also represented a new approach to city planning. It was an attempt to put architects' ideas and expertise at the service of the community, and its more disadvantaged members in particular. ■ In spite of the diversity of individual contributions, the development gives an impression of unity. The simple, clear, functional designs of the houses—flat roofs, white facades, horizontal window bands—and the attention given to integrating them into the site were hallmarks of the fledgling International Style.

Mies van der Rohe, House 3/4, rear

Hans Scharoun, House 33, entrance

The houses at Weissenhof were conceived as model homes for the Werkbund Exhibition of 1927, and built within the space of only five months (above). The architects outlined various specifications, which included the following: open floor plans rather than enclosed rooms; tenant participation in laying out the apartments, utilization of roofs as terraces; and extensive use of prefabricated elements to keep down construction costs.

Attacks from the conservative architectural camp were not long in coming. To the Nazis, the development was nothing but an eyesore, a disgrace to the country. Today, the eleven remaining, restored buildings stand as an outstanding example of modern architecture.

GERMAN PAVILION, BARCELONA WORLD'S FAIR

Architect: Ludwig Mies van der Rohe

When the architect asked his contractor what was going to be exhibited in the projected building, he was told, "Nothing will be exhibited. The pavilion itself is the exhibit." ▪ Mies was thus at liberty to design what he wanted, how he wanted. The result became known worldwide, admired and celebrated like no other structure of the period. ▪ The pavilion is actually quite small, consisting of a slab roof poised on eight steel supports to one end of a podium, accompanied by two pools. The exterior is so unobtrusive that the entrance is not immediately visible. Nor are the building's function and purpose evident from outside—everything has been reduced to essentials. ▪ The interior gives an impression of cool elegance. Exquisite materials convey a sense of luxury, and were evidently intended to impress visitors to the World's Fair.

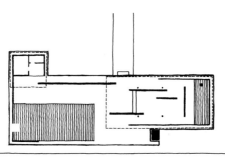

The space is defined by the dimensions of the roof slab and the panes of glass suspended from it. There are no contiguous walls, only partitions, and the roof is supported by steel columns coated in chrome. The result is an open plan with spaces that flow into one another. ▪ The walls are clad in beautifully grained marble and the floor is paved with travertine. In one of the pools, which are made of marble and are surrounded by marble walls, stands a sculpture by Georg Kolbe, *Morning*. ▪ The pavilion was dismantled when the fair came to an end, but its impact had been so great that it was re-erected and opened to the public.

MODERNITY AND NATIONALISM

The fourth meeting of the CIAM took place in July and August of 1933. Under the chairmanship of Le Corbusier and French architects, the participants addressed the topic of "the functional city," a definition of which had been reached two years previously in Berlin. They advocated dividing cities into zones corresponding to the key functions of dwellings, recreation, work and transportation. Their propositions were enshrined in the **Charter of Athens**, which Le Corbusier revised in 1941 and published, anonymously, in book form in 1943. ▪ While these developments were taking place, authoritarian regimes established themselves in several European countries, becoming synonymous with the names of their leaders: Stalin in the USSR, Mussolini in Italy, Franco in Spain, and Hitler in Germany. Persecution of political opponents and intellectuals set in. Leading architects went into exile; famous schools of architecture were closed. ▪ In Germany, where great advances in modern architecture had been made, **architecture became an instrument of political power** and, in residential building, conservatism and populism carried the day. The totalitarian Western regimes cut their nations off from further modern developments. When World War II broke out, creative minds were enlisted in the service of armament and the war effort. ▪ In other parts of the world, the architecture of the modern age continued to develop, spreading to Asia and Latin America.

VAN NELLE FACTORY, ROTTERDAM

Architects: Johannes Brinkman and Cornelius van der Vlugt

This building complex was a pioneering work of Modernist architecture. Even today—after the addition of annexes and painstaking restoration—it remains an outstanding example of industrial architecture. ■ The design was based on functional considerations. The main production areas were located in open plan spaces, while the largely freestanding facade let in ample light and air. The building's rationality derives from a logical grid system, upon which the skeleton structure was built, and from the concentration of stairwells, elevators, utilities shafts and communal rooms in separate areas. The typical traits of the International Style are in evidence: cubic volumes, flat roofs, horizontal window bands and curtain-walling.

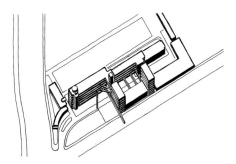

Aerial view of the plant

The three sections of the plant are devoted to different purposes, which are also reflected in their facades, yet they nevertheless form a structural and aesthetic whole. Many of the design possibilities offered by modern building methods were utilized, as in the semi-circular glazed room on the roof, which brings the overall composition to a striking culmination.

SANATORIUM, PAIMIO

Architect: Alvar Aalto

Following graduation, Aalto toured Europe, studying modern architecture. The tuberculosis sanatorium in Paimio was one of three important commissions he received in 1927–28. ■ Although the design reflects the influence of the International Style, this is functionalism with a human face. ■ In order to meet the diverse needs of the sanatorium, Aalto employed a reinforced concrete structure, which permitted an open plan. Each separate building was tailor-made to suit its particular purpose. The main building, containing patients' rooms and rest-cure lounges, faces south. The central building houses a restaurant, a library and therapy facilities. A corridor leads to the management annex to the north, with kitchen, laundry, heating plant, offices and garages. The staff and doctors' residences are separate from the hospital.

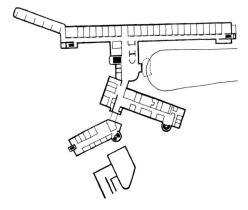

The interconnected buildings of the sanatorium splay out like a fan in the wooded landscape.

The ground plan was carefully thought out to ensure ample sunlight and air for the patients' rooms. Each function in the complex was given a slightly different form. Structural and visual order has been achieved by the use of a grid system, and the balancing of closed and open elements—solid walls and window and door apertures— is exemplary.

Many of the building's furnishings, such as the famous Paimio Chair, were also designed by Aalto, who was a gifted designer as well as an architect. His sanatorium has remained a model for hospital design to this day.

CASA DEL FASCIO, COMO

Architect: Giuseppe Terragni

The Casa del Fascio, or Fascist Party Building, was Terragni's masterpiece, and even after his premature death it remained the finest example of Italian Rationalism. Located next to the late-medieval Como Cathedral, it was intended to be one of a group of buildings surrounding a new piazza, but the others were never erected. ■ The ground plan is square, measuring 33 meters each side, and the building's height (16.5 meters) is exactly half its length. The offices lie to the outside, around a glass-roofed court-yard. The four different facades are composed in visually inter-esting variations on open and closed planes. Their proportions, like all others in the structure, conform to the Golden Section.

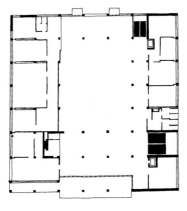

Ground floor plan

The main elevation is sheathed in white marble. The interplay of light and shade created by the inset windows and loggias produces a sense of transparency, an intentional reference to Mussolini's description of his Fascist regime as being a "glass house."

The overall impression, inside and out, is of a plain, straightforward structure, reduced to basic, almost abstract forms. A design of timeless validity despite the ideology that inspired it, the building now serves as a Casa del Popolo (community center).

TOTALITARIAN ARCHITECTURE IN EUROPE

In the 1930s, architecture in the totalitarian countries of Europe— Germany, Italy, Spain and the Soviet Union—was frequently reduced to an expression of authority and power. ■ The new, avant-garde architecture which had launched itself so hopefully into the world of the future was supplanted by an officially prescribed monumental style whose vocabulary borrowed from Classical models. Intended to impress, and intimidate, all who saw it, it was a Classicism stripped to its basic forms and blown up to a huge scale. ■ The futuristic ideas of Constructivism, Bauhaus, the International Style, the CIAM and the Charter of Athens were anathema to the totalitarian regimes. They had no place for the modern architecture that was now beginning to spread around the world.

Vladimir Shchuko and Vladimir Gelfreikh, New Lenin Library, completed 1941

Paul Ludwig Troost, Haus der Deutschen Kunst (House of German Art), Munich, 1933–37

Albert Speer, Grand Axis, Berlin, 1942

Paul Ludwig Troost, Temple of Honor
for the Dead of the Movement,
Munich, 1933–34

Albert Speer, New Imperial
Chancellery, Berlin,
1938–39

Albert Speer's plan for the redesign of Berlin epitomized totalitarian
architecture in Germany. If it had not been for the outbreak of World
War II, the capital of the Reich would have received an enormously
long and broad north-south axis (above). It was to extend from the
train station to a domed Great Hall with a seating capacity of
200,000, a building of incredible dimensions.
After 1945, the liberated nations rapidly caught up with developments in modern architecture.

FALLINGWATER, BEAR RUN, PENNSYLVANIA

Architect: Frank Lloyd Wright

This residence perfectly illustrates the interpenetration of nature and living space for which many modern architects were striving. It is a compelling example of Wright's concept of "organic architecture." The house seems to grow out of the landscape, mimicking the natural forms of the stone cliffs and ledges. ▪ The building consists of three terraces which cantilever out over the cascade. The terraces are joined to a central core made of local stone that rises from the ground like a cliff. The floor of the living area is built over a natural rock outcrop, parts of which are incorporated into the interior. The floor-to-ceiling windows heighten further this interpenetration of outside and inside. Stairs lead down to the water, whose rushing sound is an omnipresent accompaniment to life in the house.

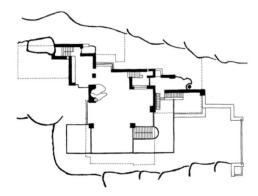

Floor plan of living area

The natural surroundings were left unaltered, and trees and bushes grow right up to the house. The colors of the concrete balcony edges and the window frames echo those of the trees and rocks. Despite its technically daring construction and the dramatic effect of its interpenetrating and superimposed elements, the building appears to be an integral part of the natural setting.

The architect was already seventy years old when he designed this house. He still had twenty creative years before him, but Fallingwater would remain his masterpiece.

DESTRUCTION AND A NEW BEGINNING

World War II ravaged cities and landscapes throughout Europe, Japan and the USSR. ■ In its wake, the world was divided into East and West. The Iron Curtain proved impenetrable to modern architecture, preventing any exchange of ideas, not to mention cooperation among architects. ■ Two camps emerged: the Western, democratically oriented world under the leadership of the United States, and the Eastern, socialist bloc dominated by the Soviet Union. In architecture, this opposition was reflected in such extreme examples as the monumental, excessively decorative style of Moscow University, and the simple, functional concrete volume of the Unité d'Habitation in Marseille. ■ Modern architecture, previously a global phenomenon, was now limited to the Western world. After the demise of communism in 1990, it became more apparent than ever how far the practice of architecture in the two camps had diverged.

TOWN HALL, SØLLERØD

Architect: Arne Jacobsen

Neoclassical architecture in Denmark was at its peak when Arne Jacobsen designed his first buildings in the International Style. His version of Modernism, however, was distinguished by national characteristics such as civic virtue and a marked regional flavor, accentuated by the use of local materials such as the Solvag marble employed as sheathing on the Søllerød Town Hall. ▪ Jacobsen's architecture has a timeless feel, due to the proportions, rigorous form and unpretentious elegance. His original application of the International Style, combined with a continuation of the Danish architectural tradition, assured Jacobsen a preeminent place among the architects of his country.

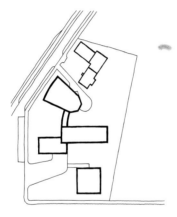

Plan of overall complex

Here a new variation was added to the many which the International Style went through. Instead of the usual white facades, the buildings have been clad in silver-gray Danish marble, and the flat roof has been replaced by a low hip roof with an attractive greenish patina. Other International Style traits remain, such as simple, cubic volumes, horizontal window bands set flush with the facade, detailed entrances, roofs and balconies, and a careful integration of the building into its surroundings. With its elegant proportions and materials, the design is simple, clear and functional.

LOMONOSOV UNIVERSITY, MOSCOW

Architect: Lev Vladimirovich Rudnev

The 1930s saw the emergence in the Soviet Union of a grandiose Neoclassical architecture that was intended to reflect the glory of Stalinism. ■ The progressive approach of the Constructivists, who in the wake of World War I had begun to develop an "architecture of the New Reality," was pilloried as "formalistic" and declined into insignificance. The totalitarian architecture that replaced it was characterized by monumentality, the borrowing of Classical elements and crude ideological symbolism. Buildings were expressly intended to embody the power, greatness, pride and permanence of the State. ■ The Soviets were so proud of their architecture that they donated it to other socialist countries, such as Poland. The Palace of Culture in Warsaw was one such "gift of the peoples of the Soviet Union." It bore strong similarities to Moscow University, and was constructed by 3,500 Russian workers in the space of three years. ■ Together with the construction of the Moscow subway, with its focus on technical perfection and an elaborate ornamentation that celebrated the country's achievements, Lomonosov University was another key landmark of the period and served as an example for many buildings in other socialist states.

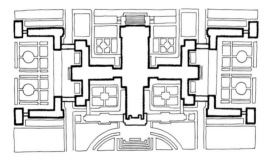

Ground plan

This gigantic complex stands on what were then the Lenin Hills (now Vorobyevy Gory), the highest point in Moscow. At its center rises a 240-meter stepped tower. Symmetrically grouped around it on both sides are further tall structures capped by towers. The eight-column portico lies on the building's axis and is itself enormous in scale. The overall impression is one of bombastic Classical monumentality. The facades are overloaded with ornament, which finds an apotheosis in statues of the Heroes of the Soviet Union.

UNITÉ D'HABITATION, MARSEILLE

Architect: Le Corbusier

The Unité d'Habitation is a seminal building in the field of collective housing. The twelve-story structure stands on two rows of massive concrete pilotis. Its 337 apartments consist of twenty-three different types which are so ingeniously interlocked that each extends from one side of the building to the other. ▪ The communal areas are supplemented by a range of public amenities, such as stores, a launderette, a doctor's practice, a restaurant, a hotel, and, on the roof terrace, a kindergarten, fitness room, paddling pool and running track. ▪ This building was the first practical embodiment of Le Corbusier's long Utopian quest for collective order and was intended as a prototype. ▪ A steel frame was originally proposed for the building, but shortages led to the use of raw, board-marked concrete, a practice which was to be widely copied. ▪ The illustration below right shows the roof terrace with its soaring, sculptural ventilation stacks.

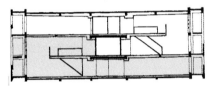

Cross-section of three floors

This typical cross-section illustrates how two apartments are interlocked to permit a central access corridor, which runs the length of the building like an interior street. The apartments extend across the width of the building, and have windows and balconies on each side. A portion of each apartment is on two levels. Since the supporting grid lies in the partition walls, the living areas are uninterrupted by supports or load-bearing walls. This permits considerable variety of layout, as exemplified in the building's twenty-three different apartment types.

GENERAL MOTORS TECHNICAL CENTER, WARREN, MICHIGAN

Architect: Eero Saarinen

Laid out around an artificial lake, the Technical Center consists of five buildings of various dimensions which house different departments (design, power plant, auditorium, etc.). None of the structures is more than three stories in height. Eye-catching accents are created by a gleaming silver water tower rising from the lake (below) and the aluminum-clad dome of the auditorium. ▪ The center was an unorthodox piece of industrial architecture for its

time, consisting of cool, crisp, refined forms. The geometric volumes of the buildings are integrated into an expansive landscaped park. The steel-grid facade, suspended from the roof beams like a curtain, is fitted with green, sun-filtering glass and black enamelled panels. The narrow, windowless ends of the buildings are clad in glazed bricks in shades of red, yellow, blue and green.

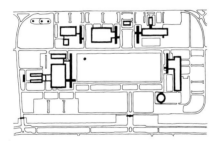

Plan of complex

This complex was an early illustration of the importance of convey-
ing a business corporation's image through architecture. The skillful
arrangement of the glass cubes and their formally and technically
refined facades gave an impression of high performance and advanced thinking appropriate to an ambitious automobile company. It
would be fifty years before the now-familiar term for this was
coined: corporate identity. This is architecture as brand image.

PEACE CENTER, HIROSHIMA

Architect: Kenzo Tange

Kenzo Tange was the first Japanese architect to achieve renown in Western Europe and the United States, thanks to this Peace Center, the design for which he presented at the eighth meeting of the CIAM in 1951. Tange's attempt to combine modern Western ideas with traditional Japanese architecture yielded unusual results that brought him international fame. ■ His admiration for Le Corbusier is evident in this complex, with its axial arrangement in the style of the Ville Radieuse, free plan, pilotis, ribbon windows and use of simple, contrasting volumes.

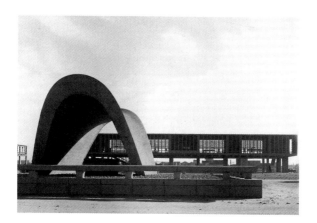

Plan of complex

The name Hiroshima has engraved itself on the history of the 20th century as the city where the first American atomic bomb was dropped on August 6, 1945, wreaking havoc and destruction, killing untold numbers and bringing illness and trauma to countless more. The Peace Park is located at the center of the former Old Town, at the site of the detonation. The site lies between two branches of the river, and is accessible by means of two small bridges and a main bridge. Adjacent to this main bridge stand the ruins of a devastated building, marking the point at which the vista through the park opens out.

The eye is first drawn to the Memorial to the Dead, whose arch is the Japanese symbol for house and grave (left). Further along the axis lies the Memorial Museum. In order to keep the vista open, the single-story structure is raised on pilotis. The museum is flanked on one side by a Community Center and on the other by a hotel (not designed by Tange).

PUBLIC HOUSING AND MODERNISM RECONSIDERED

By a twist of fate, the terrible devastation wreaked during World War II gave European architects the opportunity to start over from scratch, and the field most affected was that of public housing. ■ Following the war, hundreds of thousands of dwellings were urgently needed, especially in Germany. They had to be cheap to build and affordable to rent—an enormous challenge to the creativity and skills of contractors, architects and builders. Many specialists had been killed in the war, or had gone into permanent exile, construction businesses had been destroyed and materials were difficult to obtain, all of which considerably hampered the first years of reconstruction. As the building industry gradually recovered, German architects realized the importance of catching up with modern developments elsewhere. In 1957, at the **Interbau** building exhibition in West Berlin, architects from around the Western world erected a series of apartment buildings that set standards for public housing for years to come. ■ The same period saw the construction in East Berlin of the residential buildings on **Stalin-Allee**. These parallel projects, only a few miles from each other in the divided city, demonstrated how profound an influence ideology could have on architecture. ■ The same period also witnessed a **reappraisal of the modern tradition**, which in insensitive hands had produced crude, interchangeable buildings whose forms were dictated solely by technical considerations. This change of attitude on the part of architects led to such landmarks as Scharoun's exuberantly sculptural Philharmonie in Berlin, or Nervi's Palazzetto dello Sport in Rome, a work of engineering genius. For structures like these, forms and materials were chosen which served the task at hand, without regard to prevailing architectural trends. This period also saw the first signs of **Postmodernism**.

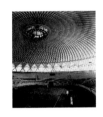

Architects: Hermann Henselmann, et al.

In 1950, Hermann Henselmann designed a nine-story residential building on Weberwiese in East Berlin. Its facade reflected the national tradition of Neoclassicism, rooted in the work of the influential 19th-century architect Karl Friedrich Schinkel, and pointed the way for architectural developments in the eastern half of the divided country. ■ The first great construction project in postwar Berlin was the development of the 1.7-kilometer-long stretch of the Stalin-Allee (renamed Karl-Marx-Allee in 1961, now Frankfurter Allee) in East Berlin. The entire boulevard was flanked by residential buildings in a uniform style, with a continuous row of shops, restaurants and other community facilities on the ground floor and apartments above. ■ No building of architectural individuality interrupted the closed ranks of the frontage, which recalled an enormous stage set for some heroic epic. This type of architecture, a version of which was prevalent in the Soviet Union at the time, contrasted sharply with Western approaches.

The entire complex was built of brick. Its concrete foundations, piers and floors were poured on site, and the facades were finished in stucco. The considerable costs and enormous time and effort entailed by manual labor on this scale prompted the development of cheaper, faster and better building methods, leading to the industrialization of the construction industry in East Germany. In 1959, a "Plan for the Socialist Reorganization of the Building Trades" was adopted. It foresaw a gradual transition to prefabricated construction in all areas of building. Soon the face of East German cities would be transformed by the repetitive grids of modular architecture.

The photograph above shows the Frankfurter Allee today. Facing page: apartment house designed by Henselmann on Weberwiese.

Architect: Pier Luigi Nervi

Nervi was a brilliant pioneer of reinforced concrete architecture. In a career stretching over fifty years, he repeatedly demonstrated his special gifts as a creative engineer and an architect of great sensibility. For Nervi, reinforced concrete was "the most beautiful structural system humanity has managed to discover." ■ The brilliantly innovative dome for the Palazzetto takes the form of a finely articulated ribbed vault. A single coffer mold, filled 1,600 times, was used to create this seemingly weightless structure. An especially elegant detail is the roofline above the ring of windows, where the roof skin ends in a wavy edge that merges into Y-shaped pilons. ■ Thanks to these thirty-six exterior supports around the arena, the interior space is free of supports. It measures nearly 80 meters in diameter and seats up to 5,000 spectators.

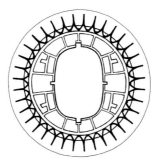

Ground plan of the arena

This small sports stadium was made possible by the use of a material of Nervi's own invention, *ferrocemento*, composed of dense concrete, heavily reinforced with evenly distributed steel mesh. The prefabricated elements were made using the technique of tensile reinforcement. To increase stress resistance, the steel armatures enclosed in the poured concrete were subjected to tension as it dried. This permitted a considerable reduction in the thickness of the elements, as seen in the present structure. A further innovation was the molding of the elements in smooth steel or plastic forms, resulting in an even, dense surface which did not require additional protection against weathering.

PHILHARMONIE, BERLIN

Architect: Hans Scharoun

By about 1918, Scharoun had shown himself to be one of the most imaginative Expressionist architects of his time. His projects, most of which were never built, were developed in numerous drawings accompanied by detailed explanations. The new Philharmonic Hall, conceived forty years later, could be traced back to a 1920 project for a community center. ■ The building is unlike anything else in modern architecture. It had no predecessors, nor did it draw on existing stylistic elements. Its sculptural form illustrates the architect's commitment to organic architecture. The importance of providing good acoustics and listening conditions for the audience were of prime concern in the design. The auditorium does indeed have superb acoustics and conveys a sense of great intimacy, enabling listeners to concentrate fully on the musical performance. The protective exterior shell built around this space is likely to appear incomprehensible to observers not familiar with the interior.

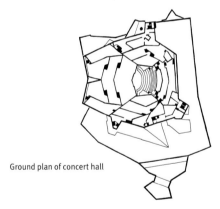

Ground plan of concert hall

The auditorium is a complex space free of supports, with the orchestral podium located at the lowest level. Around it rise tiers of seats on small, interlocking terraces, each of which can be reached from the neighboring one without using the outside corridors. No listener is more than 35 meters away from the orchestra, and the acoustics are equally good in every seat. Thanks to this close interrelationship between audience, music and space, the Philharmonie became a model for many subsequent concert halls.

INTERBAU, BERLIN

Forty-eight architects from thirteen nations, including Aalto,
Niemeyer, Le Corbusier, van den Broek, Bakema and Baumgarten

The ravages of World War II encouraged architects to explore new
solutions in architecture and town planning. Out of tragedy emerged a tabula rasa. Since reconstruction was an urgent priority, planning regulations and financial aid were required. ▪ The Interbau,
the 1957 International Building Exhibition in West Berlin, produced a remarkable cross-section of modern residential architecture
in the Western world, with several of its architects coming from
outside Europe. ▪ The first priority was to create new homes in a
time of shortage. Since public housing was subsidized by the West
German government, very tight stipulations regarding size, layout,
equipment and cost of the apartments had to be observed. This put
considerable constraints on the planners.

Imagination, creativity and a desire to exploit the best aspects of prewar Functionalist architecture led to a remarkable complex of apartment houses in the Hansa neighborhood of West Berlin. These buildings set a new benchmark and were representative of a type that exerted considerable influence on public housing schemes.
Above: The Hansa neighborhood viewed from the southeast, 1962.
Facing page: High-rise apartment building by J. H. van den Broek and J. B. Bakema.

ECONOMIST BUILDING, LONDON

Architects: Alison and Peter Smithson

This example of urban architecture is a perfect illustration of how a new, open urban structure can fit into an existing, traditional context. A new, asymmetrical city square was created, Economist Plaza, surrounded by three buildings. Ramps and stairs lead from St. James's Street to the plaza. ■ The buildings provide spaces for diverse uses: the largest one, to the rear, contains the offices of *The Economist* and the Economist Intelligence Unit; the middle-sized one was designed to accommodate stores and a bank; while a third, smaller block, next to the gentleman's club Bootles, contains apartments. The facades have reinforced concrete frames which give a vertical emphasis, while the corners were chamfered, creating the impression of wrap-around frontages. ■ The architects were at pains to ensure that their new buildings were compatible with the 18th-century scale of St. James's Street and Bury Street, and with the old London gentlemen's clubs in the neighborhood.

Building on St. James's Street

Building on Bury Street

Aerial view of complex

This project enabled the Smithsons to put into practice theories they had advanced at several CIAM meetings. They respected the established architectural setting and incorporated historical links with it into their buildings, which were nonetheless given a distinctive, instantly recognizable appearance. The architects were keen that the functions of the buildings and the methods used in their construction should be manifest in their design. The result was a group of buildings whose different forms reflect their different uses while retaining an overall visual coherence.

ARCHITECTURE IN METAMORPHOSIS

The 1960s was a decade of new directions in architecture. **Brutalism** (or New Brutalism) flourished, particularly in Britain. A style which originated in Le Corbusier's use of *béton brut* (raw concrete), it entailed the ruthless exposure of materials (precast concrete, steel, brick), structural elements and services. ■ **Structuralism** had important repercussions in contemporary architecture and urban planning. Its most salient trait was the use of a design grid, a linear network, to determine the layout of projects ranging from entire cities to individual houses. ■ Another movement that emerged in the 1960s was **Metabolism**, developed by Japanese architects with the aim of reducing the pressure on congested cities. Its adherents proposed building tower cities, creating artificial offshore islands and solving traffic problems by raising streets and railroads off the ground. Even a floating city was seriously discussed. Although these ideas remained largely utopian, a few measures were actually put into practice. ■ In the mid-1960s, the architectural tendency now known as **Postmodernism** began to emerge. It is impossible to give a precise description of this style, because the term has been applied to a wide variety of forms. Its basic thrust is the inclusion of familiar and traditional formal elements in new buildings, and a recombination of stylistic features from the past into an innovative, imaginative visual idiom.

OPERA HOUSE, SYDNEY

Architect: Jørn Utzon

Some of the most important buildings in the history of modern architecture have been the monumental structures built for the arts or for sports. When such structures are as spectacular as the Sydney Opera House, they become landmarks. With its soaring, arched concrete shells, this building has become an iconic symbol of wind-filled sails on the ocean. ■ The site is an artificial peninsula projecting into the waters of Sydney Bay. The competition called for a structure containing a large hall seating between 3,000 and 3,500 people, and a small one seating approximately 1,200 people. Utzon's entry consisted of two main sections: a plinth-like substructure several stories high inspired by the Mayan temple podium; and a roof structure made up of a series of concrete shells.

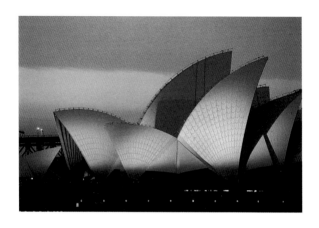

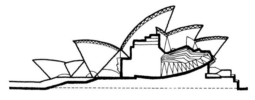

Cross section

Around 1960 a number of architects were experimenting with self-supporting monocoque concrete roofs for large halls. Utzon's distinctive design for the Opera House proved difficult to build and he was obliged to alter the geometry of the shells by giving them a spheroid profile so that they could be constructed from precast modules. Construction costs soared and the date for completion had to be repeatedly postponed. The project was also hampered by personal and political complexities, and Utzon was forced to resign in 1966. The building was finished by an Australian firm and the interior is very different from Utzon's original conception. The building now houses five auditoria, five rehearsal studios, four restaurants and six bars.

Vanna Venturi House, Philadelphia

Architect: Robert Venturi

In his 1966 book, *Complexity and Contradiction in Architecture*, Venturi presented this house, designed for his mother, as a prototype for a new kind of architecture. Venturi's aim was to get away from the rigor and high-flown claims of Modernism and to find solutions that admitted of compromise. He parodied Mies's famous pronouncement "Less is more" by retorting that "Less is a bore." He advocated an architecture permeable to both historical references and elements of mundane, popular architecture. He preferred messy vitality to unified boredom, favoring "an architecture of complexity and contradiction, which tends to include 'both-and' rather than exclude 'either-or.'" He set easily comprehensible facades composed of familiar architectural elements in front of neutral, efficiently functional volumes. He sought an architecture rooted in the American "vernacular" of the commercial strip and the suburban home. Venturi's irreverent ideas became the seed of Postmodernism, with its characteristic mixing of styles and forms.

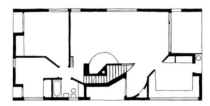

Plan of ground floor

The symmetry of the front elevation is counteracted by the different sizes and positions of the windows to the right and left of the central axis. The roof slopes up to a deep aperture on the top floor which extends to the broad chimney. On the ground floor, this aperture widens to form a loggia with the main entrance to the right. The applied stucco bands are pure decoration. The other elevations of the house have a similar design.

The ground floor is laid out along the traditional lines of American houses: an entryway with wardrobe, a kitchen with a view of the driveway and direct access to the dining room, and a separate sleeping area with bathroom. Stairs lead from the vestibule to the top floor, where another bedroom with shower is located.

ENGINEERING BUILDING, UNIVERSITY OF LEICESTER

Architects: James Stirling and James Gowan

The Engineering Building, the best-known work by the partnership of James Stirling and James Gowan, was one of the most admired designs of the 1960s in Britain. ■ With its multiplicity of forms, deliberate expression of the building's functions and complex, dynamic interplay of volumes, it marked a new direction in British architecture, away from the influences of Le Corbusier and Mies van der Rohe. The striking use of angular forms and expression of mechanical elements carry echoes of Constructivism and the work of Melnikov. ■ The architects conceived of their building "as a conjunction of fixed specific activities and of a variable changing situation." The tower at the front was designed to house the former (accommodation, lifts, staircases), while the rear was regarded as a "shed" which could be re-equipped continuously and where space could be modified as required. Both exciting and elegant, the Engineering Building had a big impact on British architecture in the 1960s.

The building consists of ground-level workshops (largely designed by Gowan) which cover most of the site, and a vertical section comprising office and laboratory towers, lecture theaters and lift and staircase shafts. The form of the tower was partly dictated by the need for a high water tank. Extensive use was made of glass (left). Indeed, to continue the idea of unbroken verticality and to create a feeling of vertigo, Stirling wanted to have sheets of unprotected glass in the glazed staircase, but he was forced to incorporate horizontal bars for safety. In addition to glass, red Accrington brick and red Dutch tiles were used for the outside (above) (the university did not want a concrete-faced building), and exposed concrete for the interior.

OLYMPIAPARK, MUNICH

Architects: Behnisch & Partners with Frei Otto and Leonhardt + Andrä

The Olympiapark in Munich was a large-scale project planned jointly by architects, engineers and landscape architects. ■ The site, bordered by the Nymphenburg Canal, had originally been a flat airfield. After World War II, rubble from the bombed city was piled here to form a hil and in 1965–68 a telecommunications tower was erected on thie site. ■ In 1966, the IOC awarded the 1972 Olympic Games to Munich, and work got under way on the new Olympic Park. The canal was dammed to form a lake, the existing hill supplemented by further ones to accommodate the buildings and sports arenas, hundreds of trees were planted, and paths and recreation areas laid out. The undulating terrain was expanded into a park which would remain open to the public after the games. Over it hovered a transparent roof of a scale and design that up until then had been restricted to the realm of the utopian.

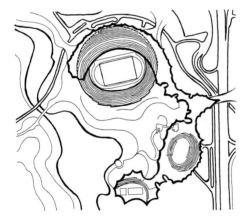

The tent-like roof is suspended from cables anchored on tall supports. The enormous loads are taken up by massive underground foundations. A transparent shell consisting of artificial glass plates lends the roof a light, airy, filigree appearance. Its gracefully rising and falling forms bordered by gently curving edges extend down to the ground in places, echoing the undulations of the sculptured landscape.

NATIONAL ASSEMBLY, DACCA (BANGLADESH)

Architect: Louis I. Kahn

Louis Kahn is a master of monumental buildings. His churches, synagogues, museums, universities and administrative centers in capitals around the world are strikingly memorable. ■ The parliament building at Dacca is a perfect example of this. By isolating it from its surroundings by means of lawns, plazas and an artificial lake, Kahn created an effect of noble detachment. In addition, its interlocking geometric volumes make the complex an outstanding example of sculptural architecture. ■ Kahn used only a small range of materials: brick for the podium and plaza paving, and roughcast concrete, finely articulated by light, together with stone bands for the buildings. ■ This extraordinary project was interrupted by civil war and changes of government, and took twenty years to complete.

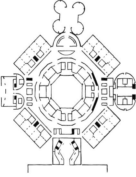

Ground plan of parliament building

The structure is characterized by variety in unity. Grouped around the central assembly hall are eight oblongs, cylinders and half-cylinders that serve variously as offices, a mosque, a school, a library, service rooms and apartments. There are no windows as such—light enters through deep apertures in the facades and is directed behind them, into the rooms. The apertures are in the form of triangles, rectangles, circles, semicircles and slits. With its alternation of solid wall and opening, cube and cylinder, the building resembles a monumental sculpture.

HIGH TECH AND TRADITION

Skyscrapers rose ever higher, and America could once again pride itself on having the tallest of all: the World Trade Center in New York. Although it would not hold the record for long, its construction set new standards, comprising a steel skeleton with a self-supporting facade 110 stories in height. Yet the world did not seem particularly impressed, perhaps because men had just landed on the moon. ■ Architects became increasingly preoccupied with expressing structures, technologies and materials by exposing and even drawing attention to them. This new style was known as **High Tech**. Ventilation ducts, piping and wiring, service and elevator shafts, steel frameworks with their rivets, and nuts and bolts, were all turned outwards, revealing what previously had been concealed within. Construction techniques became a hallmark of style. Here at last was a form of architecture that was truly liberated from historical reference. ■ Yet these halcyon years also saw the emergence of a different kind of architecture that was adapted to local and traditional needs. It resulted in unassuming designs built to a human scale that were embedded in the landscape, be it natural or man-made. Representing a return to the old and familiar, they amounted to a serious alternative to the grand designs of modern architecture. In the eyes of American architect Robert Venturi, these countless structures that are such an important part of our everyday world that we hardly even notice them represent a "competing reality."

1970–73 **World Trade Center,
New York**
Architect:
Minoru Yamasaki
Pages 120–121

1972–83 **Museum Abteiberg,
Mönchengladbach**
Architect:
Hans Hollein
Pages 122–123

1975–79 **Atheneum,
New Harmony, Indiana**
Architect:
Richard Meier
Pages 124–125

1979 **School, Broni**
Architect:
Aldo Rossi
Pages 126–127

1979–84 **Lloyd's of London**
Architect:
Richard Rogers
Pages 128–129

WORLD TRADE CENTER, NEW YORK

Architect: Minoru Yamasaki

The title "Tallest Building in the World" is regularly passed on from one to the next. For a year it was owned by the twin towers of the World Trade Center in New York, whose 110 stories rise 412 meters into the sky. Yet only a year after its completion it was overtaken by the Sears Tower in Chicago, at 443 meters. ■ The two identical towers built over square ground plans 63 meters each side lie in southwest Manhattan and are part of a group of several buildings. The site covers an area of 20,000 square meters. A further impressive statistic—the towers are occupied by 50,000 employees working for 1,200 companies involved in world trade. Access to the floors is provided by a total of 208 elevators. ■ When excavation work began in 1966, over a thousand million cubic meters of earth and rock were dumped into the nearby Hudson River, creating new land that is now Battery Park City. ■ The construction of the towers was a remarkable engineering feat. First the elevator shafts were built, then cranes erected on them to lift the prefabricated elements of the steel frame into position. As building progressed, the cranes clambered higher and higher. ■ The picture below shows a view of the lobby.

Overall site plan

Research into techniques for constructing skyscraper frames and facades is never ending. With its load-bearing walls, the World Trade Center marked a new departure from the conventional steel-frame construction. The façade is effectively a prefabricated steel lattice supporting the weight of the building and leaving the office spaces free from columns. This structure, however, resulted in windows that are only 55 centimeters wide. The alternation of pillars and windows lends the facade a smooth, impenetrable appearance. The two towers are like gigantic blocks that shoot without interruption into the sky, their angularity accentuated by the light-colored corners and roof edging.

MUSEUM ABTEIBERG, MÖNCHENGLADBACH

Architect: Hans Hollein

The Museum Abteiberg served as a point of departure for a series of innovative museum buildings in the 1980s, and it became a landmark of Postmodern architecture. ■ There was a growing realization that museums could be more than empty containers for works of art, and could be aesthetic statements in their own right. The quality of their design could reflect that of the art they housed. ■ In designing this building, Hollein took careful account of the museum's permanent collection. The design of the rooms was adapted to individual works of art, leading to a variety of spaces of different sizes and heights which were also reflected on the exterior. This diversity fits in well with the surrounding urban environment, which consists of a haphazard arrangement of small-scale buildings. Due to the sloping site and the proximity of the neighboring buildings, access to the museum is provided by three routes: up the slope and through the monastery garden, by way of a ramp leading from the town center, and via a walkway from Am Spatzenberg street.

Aerial view of site

The three access routes converge on the roof terrace, where a pavilion for temporary exhibitions, the entrance building, seven exhibition sheds, and the administrative office tower (above) are all located. The main exhibition space and cafeteria lie below the roof terrace.

The various functions of these building volumes are expressed architecturally in the different materials and forms employed. Many of the rooms are accessed from the corners. This leaves large uninterrupted expanses of wall for the hanging of paintings and the display of sculptures and provides viewers with the new experience of entering exhibition spaces on the diagonal axis.

123

ATHENEUM,
NEW HARMONY, INDIANA

Architect: Richard Meier

Richard Meier's buildings cannot easily be classified in any of the standard categories of contemporary architecture. They are reminiscent of such modernist designs as the villas of Le Corbusier or the buildings by Terragni, the Italian Rationalist, and yet they carry echoes of Postmodernism. The subtle use of apertures and hollows, the interpenetration of interior and exterior elements, and the interplay of smooth, angular, pointed and sweeping volumes form a unique, highly personal language which has a strongly sculptural quality. One of the most distinctive characteristics of his buildings is their whiteness. As he himself explained in his acceptance speech for the Pritzker Prize in 1984, "White conventionally has always been seen as a symbol of perfection, of purity and clarity ... It is against a white surface that one best appreciates the play of light and shadow, solids and voids."

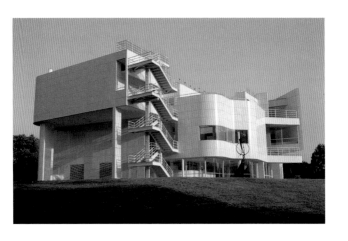

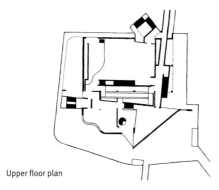

Upper floor plan

The Atheneum is a visitors' center for the historic town of New Harmony, a utopian community founded in 1825. Open on all sides, the building lies on a landfill on the shore of the Wabash River, the course of which is echoed in the curving facade. The building was designed to embody the related ideas of an architectural promenade and a historical journey. To emphasize its function as a public building, as many spaces as possible are visible and the glass walls contribute to this impression of openness. Large windows frame selected views of the town. The use of ramps, glass walls, columns and graceful curves recalls Le Corbusier's Villa Savoye. As in Meier's earlier buildings, the exterior is clad in a grid-like pattern of square white porcelain steel-backed panels.

School, Broni

Architect: Aldo Rossi

Aldo Rossi was the leading exponent of Rationalism in contemporary Italian architecture. The basic forms of his designs, as in the school in Broni, are cubes, cylinders and pyramids. It is an artful composition which revolves around the discipline of exact geometry and proportion. It dispenses with personal touches and decorative gestures, displaying a reduction of means that verges on abstraction. ▪ The play of light and shade is an integral part of Rossi's buildings. Without the intense light of southern climes, architecture of this kind would lose much of its effect. ▪ It consists of four sections containing classrooms laid out on a rectangular plan and connected by covered walkways. In the middle of the central couryard stands a two-story octagonal auditorium.

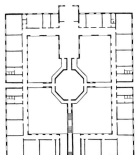

Ground plan

The overall plan was conceived according to a precise geometry. The assembly hall and walkways lie on the central axes, dividing the site into four areas. The classrooms are laid out according to a strict grid and have identical dimensions. Repetition also characterizes the doors and windows, the roof lines, colonnades and materials. The entire building has been conceived in terms of a few, fundamental elements.

LLOYD'S OF LONDON

Architect: Richard Rogers

Every interior and exterior component of this complex architectural machine was prefabricated and assembled on site. The ground plan is rectangular. The load-bearing support system, stairwells, elevators and utilities' shafts were placed on the outside of the building. This was done not only for visual reasons, but also to create an open interior space. The glazed interior atrium extends through all fourteen floors and rises above the staggered office tracts. Its finely articulated structure stands in striking contrast to the massive framework of the surrounding office floors, and makes it the culmination of the design. ■ For the maintenance of the complex metal facade, cranes have been permanently installed at several points. ■ This building has come to represent the epitome of High Tech architecture. It was designed to be able to adapt to the fluctuating needs of the underwriting business and its futuristic appearance was intended to serve as a fitting symbol for the company itself.

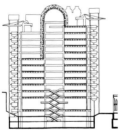

Cross section

The building's interior consists of a single, uninterrupted space with a glazed atrium 90 meters high at its center. The fourteen floors open onto the atrium and are connected by six stairway, elevator and supply structures located on the outside of the building. The five lower floors are also accessible by internal escalators.

Only the first seven floors cover the entire ground plan. Those above are set back in terraced arrangement. The resulting open areas currently serve as roof terraces, but they can be built on if required. At present over 10,000 people work in the Lloyd's Building.

BUILT UTOPIAS AND BELATED POSTMODERN HEYDAY

In an exhibition entitled "Deconstructivist Architecture" (MoMA, New York, 1988), an attempt was made to present **Deconstructivism** as the style of the future. This movement was characterized by a spectacular formal language which involved the "deconstruction" of time-tested building elements and the reassembly of the resulting fragments into apparently random configurations. Through distortion, fragmentation and the juxtaposition of jarring elements, it undermined conventional concepts of unity and harmony. It was not a coherent movement, however, and simply provided further testimony to the pluralism of contemporary architecture. ▪ In the 1980s, Postmodernism experienced a belated heyday in the form of the AT&T office tower in New York. "Now the Box Has Been Decorated," declared the headlines on the 132,000-tonne facade of pink granite. This striking edifice, with its glittering arcades of shops, atrium and monumental entrance arch, was one of the most controversial buildings of its period. ▪ While spectacular buildings like this were rising around the world, in Japan a master of tranquillity was creating an architecture of meditation. And nearby, the most gigantic construction project of the period was getting under way, an airport on an artificial island in the Pacific, built to technical standards that verged on the utopian.

AT&T BUILDING, NEW YORK

Architect: Philip Johnson

For this celebrated building, Philip Johnson, previously a distinguished exponent of the International Style, liberally borrowed from the architectural repertoire of the past to create the first Postmodern skyscraper in New York. ■ Rejecting the glass-box formula, he returned to the tripartite division of the facade typical of the tall buildings of the 1920s. The entrance is flanked by columns in the style of a Roman portico and crowned by a triumphal arch. The tower proper consists of wall slabs faced with stone into which the window apertures are cut. Articulation is achieved by means of slightly protruding pilaster bands. The attic story is surrounded by a sort of colonnade with a gallery behind it. Above this rises a roof with its distinctive broken, "Chippendale" pediment. ■ Shown below is the 30-meter-high glazed atrium on the ground floor.

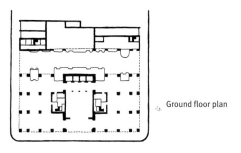

Ground floor plan

The AT&T Building (now the Sony Building) is 197 meters in height and has 36 stories, 28 of which are identical. The American Telephone and Telegraph company vacated the building soon after moving in and it was taken over by the Sony Corporation. The building itself is in fact a standard office space which Johnson has clad in a veneer of pink granite and dressed up with a number of historical quotations. Up until then, transparent, completely glazed curtain facades had been the standard for New York skyscrapers. Another unusual feature is the striking open-topped pediment in place of the usual flat roof. Every detail of the design was intended to convey status, and the building is undeniably an eye-catching presence on the New York skyline.

133

PYRAMID, LOUVRE, PARIS

Architect: I.M. Pei

The Pyramid was one of the most ambitious of the "Grands Projets" undertaken during François Mitterrand's presidency. The French Ministry of Finance was removed from the Richelieu Wing to new premises at Bercy, making possible the expansion and reorganization of the museum, and I.M. Pei was appointed to design a huge new extension. ■ Pei had the idea of locating the entrance to the museum in the middle of the Cour Napoléon and placing all the requisite spaces and facilities underground. ■ For the entrance structure itself, he opted for a light, transparent, glass pyramid. The abstract geometry of this structure does not compete with the architecture of the surrounding buildings, but rather forms a highly convincing contrast. Fears that the dignity of the existing structures would be compromised by the modern addition proved unfounded.

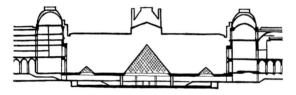

Cross section of Grand Louvre with the Pyramid

The three wings of the palace form a U-shape and each wing has a large portal at its center. The pyramid is aligned with these axes at the point where they intersect. In addition to the entrance lobby (facing page), the vast undergound precinct contains cafeterias, a shopping mall, an auditorium for the Ecole du Louvre, the research laboratory for the Musées de France, storage areas and a parking lot. Access to the three wings of the Louvre is provided by way of underground corridors.

The glass roof of the Pyramid provides an uninterrupted view of the surrounding palace buildings. Consisting of 675 rhombic and 118 tri-angular panes bolted to an extremely fine metal grid, it provides bright daytime illumination for the entrance concourse below.

Attic Conversion, Falkestrasse, Vienna

Architects: Coop Himmelb(l)au

The long-denied building permit for this project was finally granted on the grounds that it did not represent an attic conversion but a work of art. This judgement accords with the notion that Deconstructivism was concerned more with aesthetics than with architecture, with creating usable, inhabitable works of art. Its first priority was actually to attack visual habits, in a way that revealed its proponents' distaste for the conventional norms of architecture. ■ The project, built on the roof of a stately apartment building dating from the turn of the 20th century, houses an attorney's office. The conference room (below) lies beneath a great glass vault whose steel supports, ranging from the delicate to the over-massive, are interwoven into a complex, chaotic web that gives the impression of being on the verge of collapse. The flanking office spaces take on a more "normal" appearance as they approach the neighboring buildings.

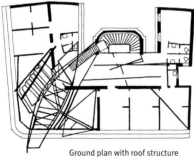

Ground plan with roof structure

The roof structure is highly unusual, consisting of a system of inter-penetrating steel and glass elements suspended from a gleaming metallic framework that projects beyond the hundred-year-old facade. This radical alteration of the existing structure is in striking contrast to the conventional attic conversions found in the neigh-borhood. Clarity, rigor and logic—not to mention the principles of structural engineering—play no role here. Through the use of superimposition, fragmentation, discontinuity, broken, sloping planes, and truncated forms, the architects have attempted to cre-ate an impression of something provisional and unstable.

Architect: Tadao Ando

Ando is known for his hermetic, introverted, meditative buildings. They are all constructed of cast concrete with the casting marks left unaltered inside and out. Their simple, lucid forms owe much to traditional Japanese architecture, while at the same time bearing traits of Western modernism. Ando's buildings have a rigorous geometry and the forms and materials he uses are radically minimalist. He restricts himself to cubes and cylinders, concrete and glass, resulting in an architecture that verges on the abstract. Illumination is achieved by an alternation of closed and open wall surfaces. Their exteriors have a forbidding appearance, and many have windowless facades. Life takes place behind encompassing walls, in a plain courtyard which, as in the case of the Church of Light, forms an oasis of calm in conjunction with the buildings of the old church. ■ Ando's architecture is imbued with the poetry of simplicity.

Plan of site

The chapel is a plain cube whose interior is divided by a diagonal wall panel that does not extend to the ceiling. At the points where the panel meets the walls, areas of glass begin. On the east side, a crucifix is incised in the concrete wall. The morning sun falls through this cross to create a second cross on the floor, a cross of light whose reflection is visible on the ceiling. As the architect himself has put it, "Light ... blows life into 'place.'"

KANSAI INTERNATIONAL AIRPORT, OSAKA

Architect: Renzo Piano

In an age that worships technology, a project as gigantic as Osaka Airport no longer seems particularly astonishing. Viewed from the air, its structures resemble a giant glider, with the terminal building as fuselage and the gates as wings. This visual analogy has become Kansai's hallmark, along with the distinctive aerodynamic shape of the roof. The latter is an irregular arch and was designed to channel air from the passenger side to the runway side and to resist earthquakes. The wings converge on a tall atrium filled with vegetation. The architect described his building as "a precision instrument, a child of mathematics and technology."

Cross section of terminal

The enormous scale of the terminal is emphasized by the statistics: 180 million cubic meters of earth were moved into the sea to create an artificial island 4.5 kilometers in length and 1.3 kilometers in width. The main building is 1.7 kilometers long and has 42 embarcation gates. Connection with the mainland is provided by a 3.8-kilometer-long bridge, for which 1,000 piers had to be rammed 80 meters down into the seafloor. Each is anchored 40 meters deep in the rock, stands in 20 meters of mud, and extends 20 meters above the waterline. The roof, 90,000 square meters in area, consists of 82,000 identical stainless-steel panels. ■ Some 10,000 people worked on the construction project. Kansai International Airport is one of the largest man-made structures in the world.

BOUNDLESS
FORMAL DIVERSITY

Toward the end of the last century, contemporary architecture consisted of a number of separate currents, some running in parallel, others intertwined, and still others having nothing in common with each other. Architecture seemed to be in a state of incessant change, with an apparently inexaustible abundance of design ideas and innovative construction techniques. Devoid of homogeneity, architecture began the new century as it had finished the previous one, with a mixture of forward-looking vision and backward-looking eclecticism. ■ In the field of public building, status-consciousness reached new levels. Large corporations, cities, states and nations basked in the light of the names and buildings of major architects. A multiplicity of projects prompted a wide range of ideas on the part of architects, leading to a stylistic pluralism which has become the hallmark of our era. ■ A part of the history of the future has already begun, in the form of **virtual architecture**, generated by the computer design programs that relieve architects from the chore of drawing and can rapidly give precise visual form to ideas. The next step will be the creation of full-scale virtual spaces which can be entered with the aid of digital technology. Conventional architectural drawings and models are becoming increasingly superfluous, replaced by projected facades one can walk along and interiors one can explore. Utopian fantasies previously thought impossible to realize because impossible to depict are now capable of being made visible. And all by the click of a mouse. The traditional profession of "architect-draftsman" has become a thing of the past, replaced by that of the "architect-programmer."

BIBLIOTHÈQUE NATIONALE, PARIS

Architect: Dominique Perrault

This gigantic complex, the last of President Mitterrand's "Grands Projets," covers an area of approximately 350 by 200 meters. The four slender, L-shaped glass towers, which rise 80 meters above the plinth, were inspired by the image of an open book. ■ It was President Mitterrand himself who selected Perrault's project from the shortlisted entries, which included a very different kind of design by James Stirling in the form of a Postmodern recollection of 18th-century French architecture. ■ In spite of the elegant simplicity of Perrault's design, the glass towers were criticized as being inappropriate for storing books, and it proved necessary to install wooden shades to shield them from direct sunlight.

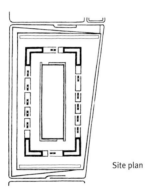

Site plan

The basic structure consists of a giant plinth with four L-shaped
towers at each corner, although much of the library actually lies
underground. The plinth is covered in wooden decking, forming a
large raised plaza. In the center of the structure lies a sunken landscaped garden which provides lighting to the surrounding floors.
The corner towers are entirely glazed but have wooden screens to
protect the books. In all, they contain 21 million books on 420 kilometers of shelves.

JEWISH MUSEUM, BERLIN

Architect: Daniel Libeskind

In 1988, the German Senate agreed to approve financing for a "Jewish Museum Department" that would remain administratively under the control of the Berlin Museum but that would have its own autonomous building. The following year, American architect Daniel Libeskind was awarded first prize in the competition. ■ The building has a basement floor, a ground floor, and three upper floors. The only entrance is located in the old Berlin Museum next door, although there is no connection above ground between the two structures. Thus the two buildings are bound together, while remaining separate—the symmetrical, rectilinear court building dating from 1735, with its Baroque facade, and the new museum with its zigzag ground plan and zinc plating geometrically incised with slits to let in light.

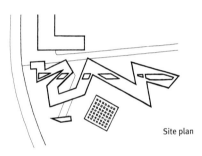

Site plan

Visual surprises await the visitor inside the museum as well as outside. The multiple angles and switchbacks of the building are intersected by an inaccessible space running along the longitudinal axis. This is the embodiment of a concept central to Libeskind's design— the void—that is intended to recall the loss of Jewish lives and culture in the Holocaust. There is a stairway that apparently leads nowhere and is overhung by heavy concrete beams that seem on the verge of crashing down, and dark corridors that end in solid walls and have floors so warped that they cause many visitors to stumble. Outside stands the Holocaust Tower, a cold, dark, windowless structure illuminated by a single small aperture high overhead. In the Garden of Exile and Emigration stand forty-nine tilted pillars arranged in a square. On forty-eight of these grow trees that stand for the founding of the State of Israel in 1948. All of these architectural features can be seen as symbols of a German-Jewish history that, broken and destroyed, has been renewed and made visible in this symbolically charged building.

Architect: Frank O. Gehry

Gehry's buildings are the product of an extraordinarily creative approach to design. Thanks to his unusual ideas and daring designs, he has become a highly sought-after architect. Many cities are keen to possess a sample of his architecture in the belief that it would attract a large number of visitors. As the architect says, "I approach each building as a sculptural object." This approach has resulted in tilted, sweeping, angular structures that are among the most unusual buildings of the late 20th century. ■ One of the principal concerns in the Zollhof project was the revitalization of the surrounding area. The scheme consists of three comparatively small buildings, each one different and each one linked to the immediate environment. Seen from a distance they merge into a cohesive architectural sculpture. ■ The distorted facades conceal relatively normal interiors. A frame construction permits the floors to be adapted to a diversity of uses. The dramatic and unconventional exterior is like a stage set intended to create an illusion, while behind it, business goes on as usual.

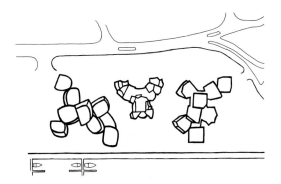

Overall site plan

The construction of this project typifies Gehry's design process. Initial drawings were followed by models. These were electronically scanned so that the data could be fed into a computer and developed further. The software used was originally designed for aircraft manufacture, and is capable of imaging complex three-dimensional bodies. The computer files were translated into real components by a company specializing in prefabricated parts. Computer controlled machines were used to mill molds for the curving facade components made out of hard synthetic polymer blocks. These were then filled with concrete, and the resulting prefabricated facade parts assembled at the construction site. The framework consisted of a reinforced concrete skeleton built on-site.

THE GREAT COURT, BRITISH MUSEUM, LONDON

Architect: Norman Foster

The Great Court is an inner courtyard at the center of the British Museum (designed in 1823–47 by Sir Robert Smirke). Measuring 96 by 72 meters, the court was originally conceived as a meeting place where museum visitors could circulate and take refreshments while visiting the extensive collections in the four surrounding museum wings. But the museum, which also served as national library, rapidly ran out of space and in 1857 the Round Reading Room was built. Gradually the rest of the courtyard filled up with outbuildings, nicknamed "the iron library" because of their iron shelves. As a result, the original focus of the museum was lost. In

1997, as the new British Library in St. Pancras neared completion, Foster and Partners started work on their scheme to renovate the courtyard and the Reading Room. ■ The photograph left is of the built Court, while the other two are virtual computer designs.

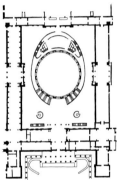

The Reading Room was converted into a new public reference library and multimedia information center. The roof over the courtyard is a latticework of steel cables made weathertight with 3,312 panels of glass, each a slightly different-shaped triangle. The panes of glass are partially covered in pale green ceramic dots, or "frits," which diffuse the sunlight. The geometry of the roof's toroidal framing was defined using a customized computer program. The junction of the roof and the Reading Room uses a ring of 20 composite steel-and-concrete columns, which align with the room's original cast-iron frame. These columns are concealed by the new limestone cladding surrounding the entire drum of the Reading Room. Two great staircases encircle the Reading Room, linking the piazza to the upper galleries of the museum. The staircases give access to mezzanine levels which accommodate various facilties, including book stores, restaurants and cafés.

THE EDEN PROJECT, CORNWALL

Architect: Nicholas Grimshaw and Partners

Harking back to the spectacular glasshouses of the 19th century, the Eden Project consists of a series of geodesic domes (biomes) which shelter plant life and ecosystems from around the world. The project is both a celebration of the natural world and an attempt to promote the responsible management of the earth's natural resources. ■ Although the geodesic dome was developed in the 1930s and 1940s by Buckminster Fuller, Grimshaw has taken the concept a stage further. The domes here are so light that the air inside weighs almost as much as their tubular framework (the Humid Tropics biome actually weighs less than the air it encloses). The structure has been designed to capture solar energy, with the back wall serving as a heat sink to radiate heat at night. ■ The building has an organic feel entirely in keeping with its function. The biomes actually appear to be growing out of the old quarry pit, and their hexagonal and pentagonal shapes echo those encountered in the structures of plants and insects.

Overall site plan

The intersecting biomes extend for 858 meters. The biggest is 200 meters long, 100 meters wide and 65 meters high. Each biome is made up of galvanized, straight sections of tubular steel, bolted together like a giant construction toy to form 625 hexagons, 16 pentagons and 190 triangles . The hollow frame of each dome has been filled with translucent, triple-layered ethylene tetrafluoroethylene (ETFE) pillows (opposite, top). ETFE is very light (one-hundredth the weight of glass), recyclable and easy to replace. It is also more flexible and less dangerous to work with than glass. The site (above), a former quarry, was uneven, unstable and prone to flooding. The quarry floor had to be raised and computer-aided modeling and manufacture was required in order to construct the frames of the biomes (each component is thus a one-off).

In the preceding pages we have given a chronological review of significant buildings of the 20th century. As the examples indicate, the past one hundred years brought a great cultural transformation in the course of which no single contemporary architectural style emerged to dominate the rest. Rather, there was a plethora of directions, trends, tendencies, schools and approaches. ■ These ultimately flowed into the loose category of "Postmodern architecture," which involved a sort of collage of elements taken from previous eras. The stylistic pluralism in architecture was mirrored in the visual arts. ■ Whether some of the buildings discussed will prove seminal to the evolution of architecture or merely reflect passing fads, only time will tell. ■ Developments in architecture and society are interlinked. Architecture does not exist in a vacuum, but must meet the social and cultural needs of people. In future, in addition to exploiting the continuing technical innovations that are likely to occur, architects will have to pay more attention to husbanding the scarce natural resources of our planet. They have a responsibility to take account of environmental and ecological factors in their work. ■ From the vantage point of today, an inexhaustible abundance of construction systems and technologies is conceivable, leading to a range of new forms and configurations hitherto undreamed of. ■ With this in mind it, is reassuring to know that architecture will nevertheless remain what it always has been—a vitally important, living form of art.

The dates refer to the commencement of projects.

1896 Amsterdam Stock Exchange by Hendrik Petrus Berlage. Glasgow School of Art by Charles Rennie Mackintosh.

1900 Entrances of Paris Metro stations by Hector Guimard. Hôtel Solvay, Brussels, by Victor Horta.

1901 Fuller Building, New York, by Daniel Hudson Burnham. Folkwang Museum, Hagen, by Henry van de Velde.

1903 Rue Franklin apartment house, Paris, by Auguste Perret. Carson, Pirie & Scott department store, Chicago, by Louis Sullivan. Larkin Company Administration Building, Frank Lloyd Wright.

1904 Central Train Station, Helsinki, by Eliel Saarinen. Garden city of Letchworth, England, by Barry Parker and Raymond Unwin.

1905 Palais Stoclet, Brussels, by Josef Hoffmann. Hochzeitsturm, Darmstadt, by Joseph Maria Olbrich. Garage Ponthieu, Paris, by Gustave Perret.

1906 Casa Milá, Barcelona, by Gaudí.

1907 Founding of Deutscher Werkbund. Singer Building, New York, by Ernest Flagg. Gamble House, Pasadena, by Charles and Henry Greene.

1908 AEG Turbine Factory, Berlin, by Peter Behrens. Robie House, Chicago, by Wright.

1899 Boer War begins. Rutherford discovers alpha and beta rays in radioactive atoms. First magnetic recording of sound.

1900 Boxer uprising in China. Sigmund Freud's *The Interpretation of Dreams* is published in Vienna. Max Planck formulates quantum theory. First trial flight of Zeppelin. World's Fair in Paris.

1901 Roosevelt elected president of the United States. Picasso's Blue Period starts. Marconi transmits telegraphic radio messages across the Atlantic.

1903 Orville and Wilbur Wright fly a powered airplane for the first time. First Tour de France.

1904 Work begins on the Panama Canal. World's Fair at St. Louis. Russo-Japanese War.

1905 Revolution in Russia. Einstein's first theory of relativity. Paul Cézanne, *Les Grandes baigneuses*. First motor buses in London.

1906 Picasso begins *Les Demoiselles d'Avignon*. San Francisco earthquake kills 700.

1907 Experimental wireless transmission by Marconi. Picasso and Braque start painting Cubist pictures. Louis Lumière discovers a process for color photography. First daily comic strip begins in *San Francisco Chronicle*.

1908 Blériot flies in an airplane from France to England. Ford Motor Company produces first Model "T."

1909 Goldmann & Salatsch Building, Vienna, by Adolf Loos.

1910 Century Hall, Breslau, by Max Berg. Post Office Savings Bank, Vienna, by Otto Wagner. Garden city of Hellerau, near Dresden, by Riemerschmid, Muthesius and Tessenow. Festival Hall, Hellerau, by Tessenow.

1911 Fagus Factory, Alfeld, by Walter Gropius. Sulphuric Acid Plant, Luban, by Hans Poelzig.

1912 Scheepvaarthuis, Amsterdam, by Johann van der Mey, Michel de Klerk and Pieter Kramer. Founding of Amsterdam School.

1914 Glass pavilion at Werkbund Exhibition, Cologne, by Bruno Taut.

1916 Huis ter Heide, near Utrecht, by Robert van't Hoff. Airship Hangars, Orly Airport, by Eugène Freyssinet.

1917 District Courthouse, Sölvesborg, by Gunnar Asplund. Het Scheep apartment block, Amsterdam, by de Klerk. Founding of Dutch group De Stijl.

1918 Ford River Rouge Plant, Michigan, by Albert Kahn.

1919 Monument to the Third International, Leningrad, by Vladimir Tatlin. Einstein Tower, Potsdam, by Erich Mendelsohn. Spangen Development, Rotterdam, by J.J.P. Oud. Founding of the Bauhaus.

1921 Chile House, Hamburg, by Fritz Höger. Haus Wylerberg, near Kleve, by Otto Bartning.

1909 Peary discovers North Pole. Futurist manifesto. Kandinsky's first abstract paintings. First commercial manufacture of Bakelite marks beginning of the age of plastic.

1910 Union of South Africa.

1911 Amundsen discovers South Pole. Der Blaue Reiter founded in Munich. Rutherford formulates theory of atomic structure.

1912 China becomes a republic. Woodrow Wilson wins U.S. presidential election. S.S. Titanic sinks on her maiden voyage. Balkan Wars begin.

1913 Suffragette demonstrations in London. Niels Bohr formulates his theory of atomic structure. Igor Stravinsky, *The Rite of Spring*. Marcel Proust, *Swann's Way*. First Charlie Chaplin movies.

1914 Opening of the Panama Canal. World War I breaks out.

1915 New Orleans jazz flourishes. Einstein, *General Theory of Relativity*.

1917 Russian Revolution. U.S. declares war on Germany. Balfour Declaration promises Jews a national home in Palestine. First jazz recordings.

1918 Armistice. Dada manifesto. Worldwide influenza epidemic begins, eventually killing 22 million.

1919 Treaty of Versailles. Alcock and Brown make first nonstop flight across the Atlantic. Rutherford splits the atom.

1922 Lovell Beach House, Newport Beach, California, by Rudolph Michael Schindler.

1924 Schröder House, Utrecht, by Gerrit Thomas Rietveld. Römerstadt Development, near Frankfurt, by Ernst May. Frankfurt Kitchen in this development by Margarete Schütte-Lihotzky. Garkau Estate, near Lübeck, by Hugo Häring.

1925 Bauhaus, Dessau, by Walter Gropius. Tristan Tzara House, Paris, by Loos. Van Nelle Factory, Rotterdam, by Johannes Andeas Brinkman and Leendert Cornelius van der Vlugt.

1926 Schocken Department Store, Stuttgart, by Mendelsohn.

1927 Lovell Health House, Los Angeles, by Richard Neutra. Rusakov Workers' Club, Moscow, by Konstantin Melnikov. Weissenhofsiedlung, Stuttgart, by Mies van der Rohe, Behrens, Gropius, Le Corbusier, Oud, Poelzig, Scharoun, Bruno and Taut. Chrysler Building, New York, by William van Alen.

1928 Town Hall, Hilversum, by Willem Dudok. Founding of CIAM.

1929 Barcelona Pavilion at World's Fair by Mies van der Rohe. Villa Savoye, Poissy, by Le Corbusier. High and Over country estate, Amersham, Buckinghamshire, by Amyas Douglas Connell. Sanatorium, Paimio, by Alvar Aalto.

1930 Empire State Building, New York, by Richmond H. Shreve, William F. Lamb and Arthur L. Harmon. Melnikov House, Moscow, by Melnikov. Tugendhat House, Brno, by Mies van der Rohe.

1920 Ghandi emerges as India's leader in struggle for independence. Earthquake in Kansu province, China, kills 200,000.

1922 Mussolini's March on Rome. Free Irish State (Eire) created. B.B.C. formed. James Joyce, *Ulysses.* T. S. Eliot, *The Waste Land.*

1923 First Labour government in Great Britain under Ramsay Mac-Donald. Sigmund Freud, "The Ego and the Id." First birth-control clinic opens in New York. Development of tuberculosis vaccine in France.

1924 Surrealist manifesto. First Winter Olympics held in Chamonix.

1925 Locarno Treaty. Franz Kafka, *The Trial.* F. Scott Fitzgerald, *The Great Gatsby.* Louis Armstrong begins his "Hot Fives" and "Hot Sevens" recordings (until 1928).

1926 Chiang Kai-Shek begins reunification of China. General Strike in Great Britain. Amundsen flies over the North Pole.

1927 Emergence of talking pictures.

1928 First Mickey Mouse films. First color motion pictures exhibited by George Eastman.

1929 Wall Street Crash. Ernest Hemingway, *A Farewell to Arms.*

1930 Amy Johnson flies solo from London to Australia.

1931 Spain becomes a republic. World's Fair, Paris.

1931   Rockefeller Center, New York, by Reinhard, Hofmeister, Corbett, Harrison, MacMurray, Hood and Fouihoux. Columbus Building, Berlin, by Mendelsohn. Atlantis House, Bremen, by Bernhard Hoetger. Swiss Pavilion, Cité Universitaire, Paris, by Le Corbusier.

1932   Casa del Fascio, Como, by Terragni.

1933   Totalitarian architecture in Germany, Italy, Spain and Russia. Daily Express Building, London, by Ellis and Clark. Publication of Charter of Athens.

1934   Penguin pool at London Zoo, by Tecton and Berthold Lubetkin.

1935   Forest Crematory, Stockholm, by Asplund. Bleachers roof at La Zarzuela Racetrack, Madrid, by C. Arniches, L. Dominguez and E. Torroja. De La Warr Pavilion, Bexhill-on-Sea, by Erich Mendelsohn and Serge Chermayeff.

1936   Fallingwater, Pennsylvania, by Wright.

1939   Finnish Pavilion at New York World's Fair, by Aalto. Town Hall, Søllerød, by Arne Jacobsen.

1942   Sao Francisco Church, Pampulha, by Oscar Niemeyer.

1943   The Solomon R. Guggenheim Museum, New York, by Wright.

1945   Unité d'Habitation, Marseille, by Le Corbusier. Eames House, Santa Monica, by Charles and Ray Eames.

1932   Aldous Huxley, *Brave New World*. Alexander Calder exhibits stabiles and mobiles. James Chadwick discovers the neutron.

1933   Hitler made chancellor of Germany. President Roosevelt introduces the New Deal. Chicago World's Fair.

1934   Purge of Communist Party begins in U.S.S.R.

1935   Italian invasion of Abyssinia. Robert Watson-Watt devises practical radar system.

1936   Spanish Civil War begins. First regular public television transmissions in the U.K. Athlete Jesse Owens wins four gold medals at the Berlin Olympic Games.

1937   Beginning of full-scale war between Japan and China. Picasso, *Guernica*. Jet engine first developed by Frank Whittle. Wallace Carothers patents nylon.

1938   Pogroms in Germany. Jean-Paul Sartre, *La Nausée*.

1939   World War II begins. Development of penicillin in the U.K. Development of D.D.T. (Switzerland). Igor Sikorsky builds the first helicopter.

1940   Battle of Britain. Trotsky assassinated in Mexico. First electron microscope demonstrated.

1941   Japan attacks U.S. at Pearl Harbor. U.S. enters war against Japan and Germany. Germany invades Russia. Orson Welles, *Citizen Kane*.

1946   General Motors Technical Center, Warren, Michigan, by Eero Saarinen. Dymaxion House, Wichita, Kansas, by Richard Buckminster Fuller. Kaufmann House, Palm Springs, California, by Neutra. Robinson House, Williamstown, Massachusetts, by Marcel Breuer. Crown Hall, Illinois Institute of Technology, Chicago, by Mies van der Rohe.

1947   Lomonosov University, Moscow, by Lev Vladimirovich Rudnev. Student Dormitory, Cambridge, Mass., by Aalto.

1948   Peace Center, Hiroshima, by Kenzo Tange.

1949   Harvard Graduate Center, Cambridge, Mass., by Gropius. Glass house in Canaan, Conn., by Philip Johnson. Apartment houses on Lake Shore Drive, Chicago, by Mies van der Rohe. Hunstanton School, Norfolk, by Alison and Peter Smithson.

1950   Notre-Dame-du-Haut Pilgrimage Church, Ronchamp, by Le Corbusier. UN Building, New York, by Wallace Harrison and Max Abramovitz.

1951   Lever Building, New York, by Skidmore, Owings & Merrill. Residential and commercial buildings on Karl-Marx-Allee, East Berlin, by Hermann Henselmann et al.

1954   Seagram Building, New York, by Mies van der Rohe. German Pavilion at Brussels World Fair, by Egon Eiermann, Sepp Ruf. Town Hall, Rodrove, by Jacobsen.

1955   Pirelli Building, Milan, by Pier Luigi Nervi.

1942   Fermi builds first nuclear reactor (U.S.). Magnetic recording tape developed.

1945   U.S. drops atom bomb on Japan. Yalta conference, beginning of Cold War. United Nations established. Nuremberg Trials begin.

1946   Civil war in China (to 1949). Beginning of Vietnamese struggle against France (to 1954). First electronic computer built (U.S.). Xerography process invented by Chester Carlson.

1947   Marshall Plan for economic reconstruction in Europe. First supersonic flight (U.S.). Jackson Pollock produces his first drip paintings. John Bardeen, Walter Brattain and William Shockley invent the transistor. Christian Dior's "New Look" collection. Beginning of MaCarthyism in the U.S.

1948   Gandhi assassinated. Establishment of state of Israel. Blockade of Berlin by U.S.S.R. begins. Long-playing record invented by Peter Goldmark.

1949   Formation of NATO. Apartheid program instigated in South Africa.

1950   Korean War begins.

1951   Color television first introduced in the U.S.

1952   Contraceptive pill developed (U.S.). Samuel Beckett, *Waiting for Godot*.

1953   James Watson and Francis Crick determine that the structure of DNA is a double-helix polymer.

1956 Philharmonie, Berlin, by Hans Scharoun. TWA Building, J.F. Kennedy Airport, New York, by Eero Saarinen. Cathedral in Brasilia, by Niemeyer and Costa. Administration Building, Takamatsu, by Tange. Mile High Center, Denver, by I.M. Pei.

1957 Interbau, West Berlin, various international architects. Opera House, Sydney, by Jørn Utzon. Childrens Home, Amsterdam, by Aldo van Eyck. Chase Manhattan Bank, New York, by Skidmore, Owings & Merrill. Medical Research Center, University of Pennsylvania, by Louis I. Kahn.

1958 Congress Building, Brasilia, by Niemeyer.

1959 Economist Building, London, by A. and P. Smithson. Palazzetto dello Sport, Rome, by Nervi. Engineering Department, Leicester University, by James Stirling and James Gowan. Vanna Venturi House, Philadelphia, by Robert Venturi.

1961 Science Pavilion, Seattle, Wash., by Minoru Yamasaki.

1962 Finlandia Concert and Convention Hall, Helsinki, by Aalto. Science Center, Yale University, New Haven, Conn., by Johnson.

1963 National Assembly, Dacca, by Louis I. Kahn. Town Hall, Bensberg, by Gottfried Böhm. Olympic Sports Arena, Tokyo, by Tange. Ford Foundation Headquarters, New York, by Roche and Dinkeloo.

1964 Plug-In City, Archigram. Habitat Housing Development, Montreal, by Moshe Safdie. History Faculty, Cambridge, by Stirling and Partners.

Edmund Hillary and Tenzing Norgay are the first to climb Mount Everest.

1955 Warsaw Pact signed. James Dean killed in a car crash.

1956 Second Arab-Israeli war. Beginning of rock and roll music in the U.S.

1957 Civil war in Vietnam. Treaty of Rome, formation of E.E.C. First space satellite launched (U.S.S.R.). Jack Kerouac, *On the Road*.

1958 Desegregation attempted in the South, U.S. World's Fair Brussels.

1959 Cuban Revolution.

1960 Sino-Soviet dispute begins. John F. Kennedy elected U.S. president. American scientists develop laser device.

1961 U.S. steps up involvement in Vietnam. East Germans build Berlin Wall. Yuri Gagarin (U.S.S.R.) is the first man in space. Structure of D.N.A. molecule (genetic code) determined (U.K.). Joseph Heller, *Catch 22*.

1962 Algeria becomes independent. Cuban missile crisis. Marilyn Monroe dies.

1963 Civil rights demonstrations in Alabama. President Kennedy assassinated. Pop art exhibition at the Guggenheim Museum, New York.

1964 U.S. Civil Rights Bill. Cassius Clay becomes heavyweight champion of the world. World's Fair in New York.

1965 Protestant Reconciliation Church, Dachau, by Helmut Striffler. Smith House, Darien, Conn., by Richard Meier. John Hancock Center, Chicago, by Skidmore, Owings & Merrill.

1966 American Pavilion at Montreal World's Fair, by Buckminster Fuller.

1967 Olympic Buildings, Munich, by Behnisch & Partners and Frei Otto. Church, Hérémence, by Walter Förderer. Hanselmann House, Fort Wayne, Ind., by Michael Graves.

1968 Centraal Beheer Office Building, Apeldoorn, Herman Hertzberger. Olivetti Headquarters, Frankfurt, by Egon Eiermann. Extension, National Gallery of Art, Washington, D.C., by I.M. Pei.

1970 World Trade Center, New York, by Yamasaki. Brion Cemetery, San Vito d'Altivole, Carlo Scarpa.

1971 Centre Georges Pompidou, Paris, by Richard Rogers and Renzo Piano. San Cataldo Cemetery, Modena, by Aldo Rossi.

1972 Abteiberg Museum, Mönchengladbach, by Hans Hollein. Museum, Takasaki, by Arata Isozaki. Bianchi House, Riva San Vitale, by Mario Botta. Frank House, Cornwall, Conn., by Peter Eisenman.

1975 Atheneum, New Harmony, Ind., by Meier. Walden Seven residential complex, Barcelona, by Ricardo Bofill.

1965 Rhodesia declares itself independent. Op art flourishes.

1967 Third Arab-Israeli war (Six-Day War). Conceptual art begins to emerge. First human heart transplant. World's Fair, Montreal.

1968 Assassination of Martin Luther King. Worldwide student protest movement. Pulsars discovered by Hewish and Bell.

1969 Neil Armstrong is the first man to land on moon. U.S. Dept. of Defense instigates feasibility study on ways of enabling computer networks to survive military attacks, leading ultimately to the Internet. Woodstock music festival. Sony Corporation introduces commercial VCR.

1970 First low-cost optical fiber.

1972 Email invented.

1973 Major recession in the U.S. Student protests against the Vietnam War. Energy crisis.

1974 President Nixon resigns following the Watergate affair.

1975 U.S. ends military involvement in Vietnam. Communists take over Vietnam, Laos and Cambodia. Apple II computer introduced. Indonesia invades East Timor. Punk band The Sex Pistols play their first concert.

1976 First supersonic transatlantic passenger service begins with Concorde.

1977 Neue Staatsgalerie, Stuttgart, by Stirling. Schinkelplatz, Berlin, by Rob Krier.

1978 Piazza d'Italia, New Orleans, by Charles Moore. Thompson Center, Chicago, by Helmut Jahn. AT&T Building, New York, by Johnson. Abraxas housing development, Marne-la-Vallée, by Bofill. House of the architect, Santa Monica, Calif., by Frank Gehry. Riola Church and Community Center, Bologna, by Aalto.

1979 School in Broni, by Rossi. Lloyd's of London, by Rogers. Hong Kong & Shanghai Bank, Hong Kong, by Norman Foster Associates, Ove Arup and Partners. State Studio of Austrian Broadcasting Co., Graz, by Gustav Peichl. Koshino House, Ashiya, Hyogo, by Tadao Ando. Transco Tower, Houston, by Philip Johnson and John Burgee.

1980 State of Illinois Center, Chicago, by Charles Franklin Murphy and Helmut Jahn. Public Service Building, Portland, Ore., by Graves. Science Center, Berlin, by James Stirling and Michael Wilford.

1981 Institut du Monde Arabe, Paris, by Jean Nouvel. Passenger Terminal, Stansted Airport, by Norman, Foster. Museum of Contemporary Art, Los Angeles, by Isozaki.

1982 Banca dell'Gottardo, Lugano, by Botta. California Aerospace Museum, Los Angeles, by Gehry.

1983 Louvre Pyramid, Paris, by I.M. Pei. Parc de la Villette, Paris, by Bernard Tschumi.

1984 Attic conversion on Falkestrasse, Vienna, by Coop

1977 Democratic election held in Spain.

1979 Afghanistan invaded by U.S.S.R. Sony Walkman introduced. British Premier Margaret Thatcher becomes first woman prime minister in Europe.

1980 Outbreak of Iran-Iraq war. Creation of Solidarity in Poland. Ronald Reagan elected U.S. president. First re-usable shuttle space flight (U.S.). First cases of AIDS identified.

1981 Prince Charles marries Lady Diana Spencer.

1982 Israel invades Lebanon. Commercial introduction of the compact disc. Falklands War. Steven Spielberg's movie *E.T.* is an unprecedented commercial success.

1984 The Macintosh computer is introduced.

1985 Gorbachov becomes leader of U.S.S.R.

1986 The Soviets launch the world's first permanently manned space station. Chernobyl nuclear power station in Ukraine is the scene of the world's worst nuclear disaster. BSE first recognized in cattle in the U.K.

1987 INF treaty between U.S.S.R and the U.S. Van Gogh's *Sunflowers* bought by Japanese insurance company for nearly $40 million.

1988 Palestinian uprising (intifada) against Israeli-occupied territories. Glasnost and perestroika in U.S.S.R. Moves to ban CFC's initiated to

Himmelb(l)au. Cité de la Musique, Paris, by Christian de Portzamparc.

1985 Wexner Center for the Visual Arts, Columbus, Ohio, by Eisenman.

1986 Galerie der Gegenwart, Hamburg, by Oswald Mathias Ungers. Stone House, Steindorf, by Günther Domenig.

1987 Church of Light, Ibaraki, Osaka, by Ando. Kunsthal, Rotterdam, by Rem Koolhaas. Centennial Hall, Tokyo, by Kazuo Shinohara.

1988 Kansai International Airport, Osaka, by Piano. Stadthaus, Münsterplatz, Ulm, by Meier.

1989 Bibliothèque Nationale, Paris, by Dominique Perrault. Jewish Museum, Berlin, by Daniel Libeskind. Vitra Design Museum, Weilam-Rhein, by Gehry.

1990 Thermal Baths, Vals, by Peter Zumthor. Waterloo International Terminal, London, by Nicholas Grimshaw. Haas House, Vienna, by Hollein. TGV Station, Satolas, Lyon, by Santiago Calatrava.

1991 Cultural Center, Nouméa, New Caledonia, Piano.

1992 Petronas Towers, Kuala Lumpur, by Cesar Pelli. Kant-Dreieck, Berlin, by Josef Paul Kleihues. Vitra Fire Department, Weilam-Rhein, by Zaha Hadid. Kuala Lumpur International Airport, by Kisho Kurokawa.

1993 Guggenheim Museum, Bilbao, by Gehry. New Trade Fair, Leipzig, by von Gerkan, Marg &

protect the ozone layer. Terrorists blow up a Pan Am jet over Lockerbie.

1989 Student demonstrations in Beijing brutally suppressed. Democratic elections for the People's Congress held in U.S.S.R. Communist regimes toppled in E. Germany, Czechoslovakia, Bulgaria and Romania. Berlin Wall demolished. Salman Rushdie condemned to death for blasphemy by Iran's Ayatollah Khomeini.

1990 Reunification of Germany. Iraq invades Kuwait. Nelson Mandela released. Hubble Space Telescope is placed into orbit.

1991 World Wide Web introduced. Gulf War between international coalition and Iraq. Maastricht Treaty approved by E.C. members.

1992 William Jefferson Clinton elected U.S. president. In 1992, at the UN Conference on Environment and Development, over 150 nations sign a binding declaration on the need to reduce global warming.

1994 Genocide in Rwanda.

1995 Bombing of the Alfred P. Murrah Federal Building, Oklahoma City, kills 168 people.

1996 BSE suspected of having been transmitted to humans who died of CJD. Dolly the sheep, first successful cloning of an adult mammal.

1997 UN Conference on Climate Change, Kyoto. Hong Kong is returned to China.

Partner. Printing building of the Western Morning News, Plymouth, by Grimshaw.

1994 Channel 4 Headquarters, London, by Rogers. Galeries Lafayette Department Store, Berlin, by Nouvel.

1995 Zollhof, Düsseldorf, by Gehry. Museum of Modern Art, San Francisco, by Botta. Research Center, Seibersdorf, by Coop Himmelb(l)au. Sony Center, Postdamer Platz, Berlin, by Murphy/Jahn. Phoenix Public Library, William Bruder.

1996 Conversion of the Reichstag, Berlin, by Foster.

1997 Federal Chancellery, Berlin, by Axel Schultes and Charlotte Frank. New Bundestag Building, Berlin, by Cie/Pi de Bruijn, Peter Busmann/Godfried Haberer, Meinhard von Gerkan/Volkwin Marg, Peter Schweger and Thomas van den Valentyn.

2000 Opening of the Queen Elizabeth II Great Court, British Museum, by Foster and Partners, and Tate Modern by Herzog & de Meuron.

1999 NATO bombs Yugoslav targets in response to ethnic cleansing in Kosovo. Euro introduced in parallel to certain participating EU countries.

2000 George W. Bush elected U.S. president.

2001 Human genome project, to determine the complete sequence of DNA in the human genome, is completed.

Blau, Eve and Monika Platzer (eds.), **Shaping the Great City.** Modern Architecture in Central Europe 1890–1937, Munich, 1999.

Curtis, William J. R., **Modern Architecture since 1900**, London, 1996.

Emanuel, Muriel (ed.), **Contemporary Architects**, Detroit, 1994.

Engels, Hans, **Bauhaus Architecture**, Munich, 2001.

Ferguson, Russell, **Am Ende des Jahrhunderts. 100 Jahre gebaute Visionen**, (exh. cat.) Josef-Haubrich-Kunsthalle, Cologne, Ostfildern-Ruit, 1999.

Frampton, Kenneth, **Modern Architecture: A Critical History**, London, 1980.

Gavinelli, Corrado, **Die Neue Moderne. Architektur in der zweiten Hälfte des 20. Jahrhunderts**, Stuttgart, 1996.

Giedion, Siegfried, **Space, Time and Architecture:** The Growth of a New Tradition, Cambridge, Mass., and Oxford, 1959.

Gössel, Peter and Gabriele Leuthäuser, **Architektur des 20. Jahrhunderts,** Cologne, 1990.

Gympel, Jan, **Geschichte der Architektur von der Antike bis heute,** Cologne, 1996.

Hitchcock, Henry-Russel and Philip Johnson, **The International Style**, New York, 1966.

Hitchcock, Henry-Russel, **Architecture: Nineteenth and Twentieth Centuries**, Harmondsworth, 1977.

Jencks, Charles, **Modern Movements in Architecture**, Harmondsworth, 1985.

Jencks, Charles, **Architecture Today**, London, 1988.

Klotz, Heinrich (ed.), **Vision der Moderne. Das Prinzip Konstruktion**, Munich, 1986.

Klotz, Heinrich, **The History of Postmodern Architecture**, Cambridge, Mass., 1988.

LeBlanc, Sydney, **The Architecture Traveler: A Guide to 250 Key Twentieth-Century American Buildings**, New York, 2000.

Midant, Jean Paul (ed.), **Dictionnaire de l'architecture du XXe siècle**, Institut français d'architecture, n.p., 1996.

Nerdinger, Winfried (ed.), **Bauhaus-Moderne im Nationalsozialismus. Zwischen Anbiederung und Verfolgung**, Munich, 1993.

Noever, Peter (ed.), **Architecture in Transition: Between Deconstruction and New Modernism**, New York, 1997.

Pearman, Hugh, **Contemporary World Architecture**, London, 1997.

Pevsner, Nikolaus, **An Outline of European Architecture**, Harmondsworth, 1990.

Pevsner, Nikolaus, Hugh Honour, and John Fleming, **Penguin Dictionary of Architecture and Landscape Architecture**, Harmondsworth, 2000.

Raeburn, Michael (ed.), **Architecture of the Western World**, New York, 1982.

Reichold, Klaus and Bernhard Graf, **Buildings that Changed the World**, Munich, 1999.

Schneider, Romana, Winfried Nerdinger, and Wilfried Wang (eds.), **Architektur im 20. Jahrhundert: Deutschland**, Munich, 2000.

Steele, James, **Architecture Today**, London, 1997.

Thiel-Siling, Sabine (ed.), **Icons of Architecture: the Twentieth Century**, Munich, 1998.

Thomsen, Christian W., **Visionary Architecture: From Babylon to Virtual Reality**, Munich, 1994.

Trachtenberg, Marvin and Isabelle Hyman, **Architecture from Prehistory to Post-modernism. The Western Tradition**, New York, 1986.

Venturi, Robert, **Complexity and Contradiction in Architecture**, New York, 1966.

Wiseman, Carter, **Shaping a Nation: Twentieth-Century American Architecture and its Makers**, New York, 1998.

Yarwood, Doreen, **The Architecture of Europe: the Nineteenth and Twentieth Centuries**, London, 1991.

Zukowsky, John (ed.), **Chicago Architecture 1872–1922: Birth of a Metropolis**, Munich, 1987.

Zukowsky, John (ed.), **Chicago Architecture and Design 1923–1993: Reconfiguration of an American Metropolis**, Munich, 1993.

Photographic Acknowledgments

Agenzia Fotografica Luisa Ricciarinip. 127 (Roberto Schezen)
all Over p. 109 (Tom Weber), p. 121 (Rainer Grosskopf)
Arcaid p. 105 (Martin Jones)
Archiv für Kunst und Geschichte, Berlin p. 24 left, p. 53 (Hilbich)
Kazi Khaleed Ashraf p. 116 above
Artephot p. 88 left (Maurice Babey)
artur pp. 24 right, 28 right, 54, 55, 56, 68 (2), 69, 77 (Klaus Frahm), p. 63 (Thomas Riehle)
Atelier Klaus Kinold pp. 28 left, 62, 74
Bauhausarchiv, Berlin pp. 27 left, 52 (Lill)
Jordi Bernadó pp. 84 (2), 85
Bildarchiv Foto Marburg pp. 41, 44, 57, 114 above
Bitter + Bredt p. 147
Michael Carapetian p. 104 right
Helge Classen pp. 27 right, 66 (2)
Jan Derwig pp. 37, 72
Edifice pp. 50–51 (Philippa Lewis), p. 112–113 (Gillian Darley)
Deutsche Fotothek, Dresden pp. 45
Sibylle Fendt p. 102
Georges Fessy p. 145
Foster and Partners pp. 150 below, 151
Christian Gahl p. 97
Government Printing Office Collection, State Library of New South Wales p. 108
Rena Gunay pp. 29 left, 116 below, 117
Markus Hilbich p. 100
Atelier Hans Hollein pp. 122, 123 (Georg Riha)
Sascha Jaeger p. 148
Japan Architect Co. p. 141 (Shinkenchiku-Sha)
Architektur-Bilderservice Kandula pp. 38, 39 (Günter Lachmuth)
Herbie Knott pp. 152–153
Ian Lambot p. 31 right
Landesarchiv Berlin p. 103
Landesbildstelle Württemberg,Stuttgart p. 67
LOOK pp. 120, 124, 125, 128, 129, 132, 133 (Christian Heeb)
Mitsuo Matsuoka pp. 138 (2), 139
Thomas Mayer p. 149
Grant Mudford p. 64
Stefan Müller p. 146
Osamu Murai pp. 92, 93
Museum of Finnish Architecture p. 75 (Jussi Tiainen)
Nederlands Architectuurinstituut, Amsterdam p. 73
Nederlands Architectuurinstituut, Rotterdam/Stichting Wonen Archiv p. 36
Nervi Archive, University of Parma p. 98
Frank den Oudsten pp. 26 left, 60, 61
Pei Cobb Freed & Partners p. 134, 135 (Koji Horiuchi)
Renzo Piano Building Workshop p. 140 (K. Hiwatashi)
Post Office Savings Bank p. 48 (Ellert), p. 49 (Doris Herrlinger)
Christian Richters pp. 32 left, 144

Karsten de Riese p. 144 below
Paul Rocheleau pp. 2, 80 (2), 81
François René Roland p. 42
Venturi, Scott Brown and Ass. p. 110, 111 (Rollin La France)
Jost Schilgen p. 115
Julius Shulman p. 65
Snoek p. 104 left
Stiftung Archiv der Akademie der Künste, Berlin p. 29 right (Karl E. Jacobs)
VIEW Pictures pp. 33, 101 (Dennis Gilbert)
Sybolt Voeten pp. 30 left
Nigel Young p. 150 above
Gerald Zugmann pp. 136, 137

For Irina, Thomas and Benjamin

Prestel-Verlag
Mandlstrasse 26
D-80802 Munich
Germany
Tel.: (89) 38-17-09-0
Fax: (89) 38-17-09-35
www.prestel.de

4 Bloomsbury Place
London
WC1A 2QA
Tel.: (020) 7323 5004
Fax: (020) 7636 8004

175 Fifth Avenue, Suite 402
New York
NY 10010
Tel.: (212) 995 2720
Fax: (212) 995 2733
www.prestel.com

Library of Congress Control Number: 2001092005

Prestel books are available worldwide. Please contact your nearest bookseller or any of the above addresses for information concerning your local distributor.

Translated from the German by John W. Gabriel
Copy-editing, adaptation, and entries on Letchworth, Leicester Engineering, and the Eden Project: Bernard Wooding
Picture research: Irene Unterriker
Design: Dorén und Köster, Berlin
Production: Ulrike Schmidt, Gunta Lauck, Munich
Origination: ReproLine, Munich
Printing and binding: Graspo, Zlín
Printed in Czech Republic

ISBN 3-7913-2586-8